CRIMINAL JUSTICE

Trials and
the Courts

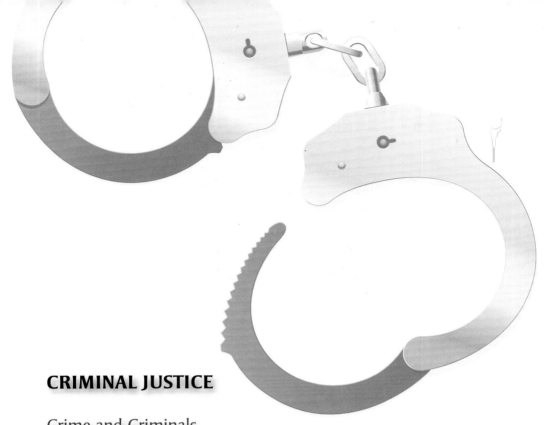

CRIMINAL JUSTICE

Crime and Criminals

Crime Fighting and Crime Prevention

Evidence

The Law

Prison and the Penal System

Trials and the Courts

CRIMINAL JUSTICE

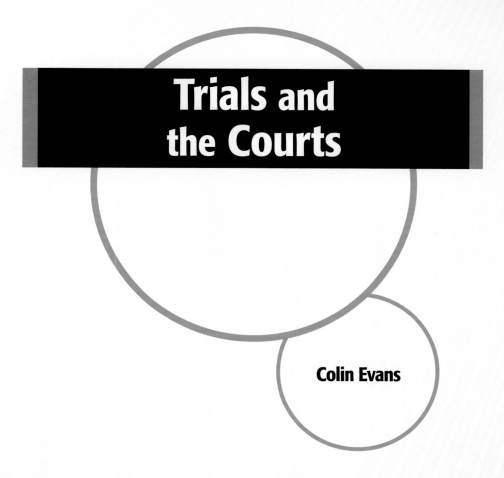

Trials and the Courts

Colin Evans

CHELSEA HOUSE
PUBLISHERS
An imprint of Infobase Publishing

CRIMINAL JUSTICE: Trials and the Courts

Chelsea House
An imprint of Infobase Publishing
132 West 31st Street
New York NY 10001

Library of Congress Cataloging-in-Publication Data
Evans, Colin, 1948-
Trials and the courts / Colin Evans.
p. cm. — (Criminal justice)
Includes bibliographical references and index.
ISBN-13: 978-1-60413-616-6 (hbk. : alk. paper)
ISBN-10: 1-60413-616-2 (hbk. : alk. paper) 1. Criminal justice,
Administration of—United States. I. Title. II. Series.
KF9223.E936 2010   345.73'05—dc22
2009047358

Chelsea House books are available at special discounts when purchased
in bulk quantities for businesses, associations, institutions,
or sales promotions. Please call our Special Sales Department
in New York at (212) 967-8800 or (800) 322-8755.

You can find Chelsea House on the World Wide Web at http://www.chelseahouse.com

Text design by Erika K. Arroyo
Cover design by Keith Trego
Composition by EJB Publishing Services
Cover printed by Bang Printing, Brainerd, MN
Book printed and bound by Bang Printing, Brainerd, MN
Date printed: April 2010

Printed in the United States of America

10 9 8 7 6 5 4 3 2 1

This book is printed on acid-free paper.

All links and Web addresses were checked and verified to be correct at the time of
publication. Because of the dynamic nature of the Web, some addresses and links may
have changed since publication and may no longer be valid.

Contents

Introduction

On the afternoon of June 15, 1215, a small band of rebellious English barons changed the course of history. They performed this feat in unlikely surroundings: a sleepy meadow known as Runnymede that lies on the River Thames between Windsor and Staines. The barons had an appointment that day with the most powerful man in England, King John, a hugely unpopular ruler who had almost bankrupted his nation in a war with France. John's ruinous taxes and flagrant disregard for the law or custom had finally stung the noblemen into action. They brought with them to Runnymede a document called *The Articles of the Barons*. It contained a list of demands, most of which were intended to demonstrate that nobody—not even a king—was above the law. John grudgingly affixed his seal to the document, which became known as Magna Carta (Great Charter), and promptly ignored its terms completely. But his death one year later revived Magna Carta and by 1225 it had become part of the permanent law of the land. Buried deep within this densely worded document lies a single clause that reads: "No freeman shall be taken, imprisoned . . . or in any other way destroyed . . . except by the lawful judgment of his peers, or by the law of the land." From these few words came one unalterable entitlement that has endured through almost 800 years: the right to a trial.

So fundamental has this concept been to Western justice that in 1957 the American Bar Association acknowledged the debt American law and constitutionalism owed to Magna Carta by erecting a monument at Runnymede. Elsewhere, there are echoes of Magna Carta in

(continues on page 10)

THE GRAND JURY

For centuries the grand jury has been an integral part of the trial process. Its origins can be traced back to the *Assize of Clarendon* in 1166. Through the grand jury, laypersons participate in bringing suspects to trial. It examines accusations against persons charged with crime and, if the evidence warrants, makes formal charges on which the accused persons are later tried. (Initially, the grand jury had dual functions; it not only accused suspects, it also tried them. Later these roles were separated.) The grand jury's function is to decide whether there is **probable cause** to believe that a person has committed a crime. There is no attempt at this time to decide guilt or innocence. That responsibility rests solely with the **petit** or trial jury.

A grand jury usually consists of between 12 and 23 persons, chosen at random from a preapproved panel. Like a trial jury, its members are sworn in and usually elect a foreman. Various public officials, such as a district attorney or a sheriff, provide information and summon witnesses for the grand jury. Its power over witnesses resembles that of a trial court. Witnesses must appear and, usually, must testify. Refusal may constitute contempt. Examination of witnesses is at the jury's discretion and need not involve the prosecutor, who cannot in any event interfere with deliberations and voting. Ordinarily, suspects may not call witnesses, present evidence, or appear before the jury.

Unlike the trial itself, grand jury hearings are usually held in secret. A grand jury enjoys far greater independence than its trial counterpart. It is instructed by the court on matters of law, and although the jury works with the prosecutor, it is not under his control. But in practice this hasn't always been the case.

Once all the evidence has been heard, the jury debates its verdict, and the choice is stark: Is there, or is there not, sufficient evidence to warrant further criminal proceedings against the suspect? Unlike its trial counterpart, the grand jury needs only to reach a simple majority. In a 23-person jury, a majority of 12-11 carries just as much legal weight as a unanimous verdict. If the jury decides that there is sufficient evidence to proceed, an indictment, which is a formal announcement of criminal charges, is returned against the suspect and the accused must stand trial before a trial jury. If the grand jury decides, however, that the state has failed to make its case, the suspect is absolved. It should be noted that the constitutional protection against **double jeopardy** that applies to a defendant in a jury trial does not hold in the grand jury. If compelling new evidence against a previously absolved suspect comes to light, a prosecutor can, and often does, return to the grand jury to seek an indictment. Whatever the outcome of the grand jury's deliberations, minutes of the proceedings are usually made available to the prosecutor and the court, and sometimes to the accused.

The grand jury's original purpose was to prevent oppressive prosecution by the English crown, by granting the citizen the right to hear charges before an actual prosecution was underway. In practice, grand juries have tended overwhelmingly to rubber-stamp the wishes of prosecutors. In some jurisdictions, certain prosecutors have been known to stack the grand jury deck by loading the panel with jurors who have a proven track record of delivering verdicts favorable to the state. This perceived bias, allied to the high costs of court hearings, has gradually eroded the use of grand juries in recent decades. At one time, the grand jury system was ubiquitous throughout the English-speaking world; now it is largely confined to the United States. Even here its impact is lessening. Although the Fifth Amendment to the United States Constitution requires a grand jury indictment for all federal criminal charges, waivers are frequent, and most prosecutions are initiated by prosecutors. It is a similar story at the state level. About half the states no longer actively employ the grand jury system, preferring instead to allow prosecutors to authorize indictments.

(continued from page 7)

the Bill of Rights, the **Fifth Amendment**, which guarantees that "No person shall . . . be deprived of life, liberty, or property, without due process of law."

In this instance, "**due process** of law" begins with a decision to prosecute. And for that to occur, a formal accusation has to be made. Typically, it is the public prosecutor who, on the basis of the results of the investigation, determines whether to proceed and for which offense to bring charges. Private citizens, such as the victim of the offense, are not generally permitted to institute a criminal action, though the law on this point differs among jurisdictions. In the United States it is practically impossible for a private individual to launch a criminal action. (Other countries, most notably England, do permit private criminal proceedings, but only rarely and always under the crown's watchful eye. At any time the state can intervene, either taking over the prosecution or discontinuing it if deemed appropriate.)

During the investigative stage, relevant evidence is collected and preserved for a possible trial. The suspect also has the right to collect evidence in his favor. In some European countries, the defendant can request the investigating authority to assist him in this endeavor. This is not the case in America, where the defendant is very much on his own. He is expected to take the initiative in preparing the case for his defense. What form that defense takes depends on his pocketbook. If he's wealthy, he can hire the very best criminal lawyers available and might even be able to outgun the state when it comes to expert witness firepower. If he's at the bottom of the economic scale, he'll get a public defender. This lawyer appointed by the state may be conscientious, no doubt, but is often staggering under an impossibly heavy caseload and without the time or the financial resources available to the prosecution.

Because of this perceived imbalance in favor of the state, the statute books do even up the playing field somewhat by imposing very strict laws regarding criminal procedure. These regulate the modes of apprehending, charging, and trying suspected offenders; the imposition of penalties on convicted offenders; and the methods of challenging the legality of conviction after judgment is entered. Arriving at this level of legal sophistication in America did not happen overnight.

Since the constitution of the United States was ratified in June 1788, everyone—the executive, the legislature, and the judiciary—has, it seems, taken a hand in trying to fashion some kind of legal order out of chaos. Someone certainly needed to, because early American justice was rough. Especially out west. Here, courts were scarce and lynchings

A REASONABLE DOUBT

The United States employs what is know as the adversarial system of justice. It has but one function: to determine whether the accused is guilty of the crime charged. Unlike some European judicial codes, there is no burden on the American adversarial system (or that of England, from which it largely derives) to determine who actually committed a crime. All that matters is the guilt or innocence of the accused. In order to prove its case, the prosecution must introduce sufficient legally admissible evidence to satisfy a jury—beyond a reasonable doubt—that the defendant committed the crime he or she is charged with. Reasonable doubt is an often misunderstood concept. Many think it means beyond all doubt. This is not the case. Reasonable doubt is the doubt that a reasonable person might be expected to entertain about a defendant's guilt.

For example, two eyewitnesses might claim they saw a suspect fleeing the crime scene. This, the prosecution admits, is the only hard evidence against the accused. Therefore, the court needs to examine closely the circumstances of that flight. If the eyewitnesses were standing a couple of yards away and it was broad daylight, then their identifications might be considered good evidence. On the other hand, if the crime took place on a poorly lit street at midnight and the witnesses were some 50 yards distant, what weight then should the jury give this testimony? Because the fallibility of eyewitness testimony is now so well documented, in this circumstance most fairminded jurors would probably lean toward an acquittal based on reasonable doubt.

were commonplace. Trials, when they did take place, were quick, often ending in less than a day, and the sentences were harsh in the extreme. And yet, when it came to integrating women into the legal system it was the frontier states that led the way. In 1870 Wyoming, having already become the first jurisdiction in the world to grant women the right to vote in all elections, further made history by being the first state to allow women to sit on juries. At the other end of the scale, Mississippi continued to bar women from jury service until 1970, "to protect them . . . from the filth, obscenity, and noxious atmosphere that so often pervades a courtroom during a jury trial."[1] (Curiously enough, such sensitivity didn't extend to female lawyers, who had been admitted to the Mississippi bar half a century earlier.) Gradually, most of these inequities were ironed out, and by the beginning of the 20th century the modern trial had evolved.

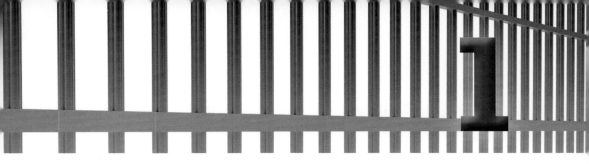

The History of Trials

The noble intentions of Magna Carta might have laid down the ground rules for trial by jury, but there was nothing at all noble about what form that trial should take. Since the early Middle Ages guilt had mainly been decided through a process known as trial by ordeal. This was not justice for the fainthearted. It was crude, brutal, and wholly lacking in the use of evidence to prove guilt or innocence. It involved forcing the accused to perform some excruciating, often disfiguring task such as plunging his or her hand into a vat of scalding oil or maybe a fire. Once the hand was withdrawn, official observers, usually priests, would then study the wounds closely, noting their severity. The wounds were then treated. Three days later the bandages were removed. If the wounds showed clear signs of healing, this was interpreted as evidence of divine intervention; and since God was unlikely to align Himself with a guilty party—so the priests averred—the accused was declared innocent. By contrast, no discernible improvement in the wounds meant that the accused was deemed guilty and subject to whatever punishment the law decreed. Very few suspects ended up in the "innocent" column.

Fifty years before Magna Carta, in 1166, King Henry II had attempted a minor overhaul of English criminal law with a series of ordinances that became known as the *Assize of Clarendon*. This established the grand jury, which was to inform the king's judges of the most serious crimes committed in each local district and to name "any man accused or notoriously suspect of being a robber or murderer or thief."[1] Like many well-meaning pieces of legislation, *Clarendon* failed to address the abuses it sought to remedy and actually muddied the waters. Its most significant outcome was a huge increase in the number of false accusations with many resulting miscarriages of justice. A decade later it was amended by the *Assize of Northampton*.

None of the pieces of legislation made much impact on the day-to-day administration of law. Trial by ordeal would remain a staple of most European judicial codes until the end of the 13th century. For a brief while thereafter, a new device, trial by combat, gained favor, especially in the upper echelons of society. This harked back to chivalric times, when knights in armor would duel on the battlefield. Trial by combat was essentially a duel, with victory and the court's verdict going to the skilled, more powerful adversary. This time, so the reasoning went, God would side with the strong. The flaws inherent in this code were too obvious for the idea to survive, and, gradually, the authorities warmed to the concept of trial by jury. But it was a case of one step forward, two steps back. Because such store was set in the confession—it was considered by far the strongest evidence—the authorities spent their time dreaming up ever more cruel and imaginative means of obtaining that confession. Suspects found themselves subjected to the most hideous forms of torture, all in the name of justice, and all designed to loosen reluctant tongues. For many, the hangman's noose or the headsman's block came as welcome respite from this state-sponsored sadism. They couldn't die quickly enough. Fortunately, there were enough progressive minds about to eventually wean society off this form of extreme cruelty, and, by the beginning of the 17th century, the notion of trial by jury was well established in England.

This was this judicial code that the Pilgrims brought with them when they arrived in America in 1620. There was just one problem: They were still subject to colonial charters. And although these conferred on them the traditional legal rights enshrined in Magna Carta, such as **habeas corpus** and the right to a trial before a jury of one's peers, in reality the new colony had few judges, lawyers, or law books. Even more galling was the fact that the most important cases were still decided in England. The sluggishness of transatlantic voyages meant that court decisions were terribly slow to reach the New World. These

An executioner puts a noose on Bridget Bishop, the first woman executed on charges of witchcraft in Salem in 1692. The Salem witch craze is a disturbing example of mob justice at the expense of sound legal reasoning. *Briggs Co./George Eastman House/ Getty Images*

delays only bred frustration and resentment. All the colonies were keen to flex their legal muscles, and steadily they chipped away at the English influence, passing their own statutes and establishing their own courts. With Massachusetts and Pennsylvania at the helm, the colonies took the view that English laws passed since the days of Plymouth Rock did not automatically apply in the colonies, and even some of the older statutes were liable to adaptation. Nor did they necessarily regard English cases as binding **precedents**.

By the late 17th century, lawyers were beginning to practice in the colonies. Some of the law, though, was still pretty rugged, to say the least. The ghastly events of Salem witch trials in 1692 demonstrated the need for a complete break with the past. All through the 18th century

(continues on page 18)

"THE DEVIL . . . BID ME SERVE HIM"

When the first Puritan settlers arrived on American shores in the early 17th century, they brought with them a desire for religious freedom. They also imported a strong belief in the power of witchcraft. This wasn't surprising. In the Europe they'd left behind, fear of the supernatural was the norm, leading to thousands being condemned to death on charges of being in league with the devil, and the settlers were reluctant to abandon the old ways. The first recorded execution in America for witchcraft occurred in 1647 in Hartford, Connecticut. Mostly, though, the religious fanaticism was low-key until 1692. That was the year when two young girls who lived in Salem Village, Massachusetts, suddenly began acting in a bizarre fashion, falling into trances, and spouting unintelligible gibberish. Soon, other local girls began exhibiting similar symptoms. A doctor who was summoned could offer only one diagnosis: witchcraft.

Something, or someone, supernatural had clearly afflicted the girls, so it was believed, and the search was on to find the culprit. Under pressure, the girls named three local women as being the source of their distress: Tituba, a slave who dabbled in fortune-telling; Sarah Good, a homeless beggar; and a widow named Sarah Osburn, who was distrusted in the local community because she had not attended church in more than three years (coincidentally she was also mired in a legal dispute with a wealthy local family, the Putnams, whom some suspect of having engineered her downfall).

The interrogators concentrated their efforts on Tituba. At first she denied any kind of supernatural involvement. Then the inquisitors reached for a whip. Under its stinging lash, Tituba's imagination went into spectacular overdrive. The accusations and fabrications spilled from her in a torrent. She denounced numerous other women in the parish, accusing them of engaging in witchcraft, and she spoke of seeing ghostly visions that included "two Catts, one Red, another black as bigge as a little dogge,"[2] and various other apparitions. Sarah Osburn, she said, had invoked her devilish enterprises by calling on some creature with "wings & two Leggs & a had [head] like a woeman."[3] Tituba's revelations, which became more outlandish by the day, caused panic in the village. An estimated 150 women, and the occasional man, were rounded up like cattle and accused of witchcraft.

Their trials began in June 1692, the start of a three-month long reign of terror. Hysteria took the place of evidence as patently innocent people were condemned to death on rumor and pure spite. By the time that dreadful summer was over, 19 "witches"—Sarah Good among them—had been hanged on Gallows Hill, Salem. Another man, Giles Corey, had been pressed to death with heavy rocks, as interrogators tried to force him to confess. He died in silence. At least four others—including Osburn, who was neither tried nor indicted—died in prison. Although Tituba did spend some time in jail, she was released. Her fate thereafter is unknown.

The madness couldn't endure forever and, soon, disquiet at the mass executions turned to disgust, and then to open revulsion. It was as if the residents of Salem had woken up from a terrifying nightmare. An influential Massachusetts cler-gyman, Increase Mather, publicly declared his opposition to the witch hunt with the famous phrase, "It were better that ten suspected witches should escape than one innocent person should be condemned."[4] The chorus of disapproval was taken up by the state governor, William Phipps, whose own wife had been denounced in the madness. Phipps acted to overhaul the trial procedure, banning the admission of so-called **spectral evidence**, and eventually pardoning all those who remained in jail.

The events in Salem in 1692 are a terrible reminder of the dangers that lie in wait for any society that abandons sound legal judgment and falls into the trap of mob justice. The only grain of comfort that can be taken from it is that the legal sys-tem listened and learned. Slowly—sometimes too slowly—the American trial system began inching toward the standard that is taken for granted today.

(continued from page 15)
discontent was mounting, and many hard-fought legal battles were waged with England in the years preceding the American Revolution.

The newly independent United States of America saw a surge in the number of lawyers (half the signatories of the Declaration of Independence were attorneys). Then, as now, most lawyers dealt with civil matters, but America was in the throes of an enormous transition. Much of this had to do with where people lived. In the early 19th century, 94 percent of Americans worked the land in rural areas. One hundred years later the demographic balance had begun to shift, with some 40 percent of the population now living in cities.[5] This urbanization might have been the engine room for America's huge economic growth in the 19th century, but it created a whole new set of sociological headaches. Chief among these was a dramatic increase in the amount of crime. And that led inevitably to more trials.

Lawyers—at least the talented ones—now realized that a very handsome living could be made from defending accused prisoners. Some of these attorneys would go on to become household names, though not always for the right reasons. New York was home to two of the earliest legal superstars. When William Howe and Abraham Hummel joined forces at the end of the 19th century, they speedily compiled a client list that read like a *Who's Who* of the Manhattan underworld. At one time, out of 25 persons accused of murder and held in the Tombs Prison, 23 listed Howe and Hummel as their attorneys. Howe was the mouthpiece, Hummel the brains (he was reputed to have been the original source for the old joke that goes, "There are two kinds of lawyers; those who know the law and those who know the judge.") To be fair to Hummel, it should be stated that this aphorism has many claims to authorship, but it certainly described his company's somewhat freewheeling legal style. Bribery, corruption, crooked retainers, **suborning** perjury (persuading others to give false testimony), nothing was out of bounds for this imaginative twosome. Between them they knew how to play every trick in the legal book. Their notoriety spread like wildfire through the New York legal system, and there it would have remained had it not been for a hugely significant improvement in the American educational system. For the first time in history, a majority of Americans could read, and they were hungry for the written word. Newspapers mushroomed, especially in the large metropolitan areas, and press barons like William Randolph Hearst and Joseph Pulitzer were quick to grasp the fact that few stories boosted circulation figures quite like a lurid murder trial.

THE SUPREME COURT

The Supreme Court is the highest judicial body in the United States. It acts as the final court of appeal in federal cases, and serves as the maintainer and final arbiter of the United States Constitution. It was instituted by the Constitution of 1787. The size of the court is set by Congress, and during the 19th century it varied from six to 10 members, before stabilizing in 1869 at nine. This consists of a chief justice and eight associate justices. The first chief justice was John Jay, appointed in 1789. Since that time 108 men have served on the court, and three women. The most recent appointee is Sonia Sotomayor, whose term of active service began on August 8, 2009.

Appointments to the Supreme Court are made by the president with the advice and consent of the Senate. Those appointed retain the position for life or until they decide to retire. The only other ground for removal is **impeachment**. Only one justice, Samuel Chase, has been impeached, for allegedly letting personal bias affect his court judgments (he was acquitted in 1805), and only one justice, Abraham Fortas, has been forced to resign (in 1969, for his outside financial dealings).

In many respects the Supreme Court is the heartbeat of the nation. It serves to clarify, refine, and test the philosophic ideals written into the Constitution and translate them into working principles for a federal union under law. These principles may change as society changes. Although the Supreme Court is a highly politicized body and its actions have frequently infuriated or dismayed large sectors of the population, by and large it is an accurate barometer of the national mood. While it has never shirked controversy, and it is unlikely to do so in the future, the Supreme Court remains the individual's best hope of protection against the whims of an oppressive government.

Reporters were dispatched in droves to cover the big cases of the day. Each morning millions of Americans would digest the previous day's legal events over their breakfast. Most had never seen the inside of a courtroom and these reports, often running to many thousands of words each day, provided their first experience of how a trial worked. They came to recognize the names of the great trial lawyers. These were the characters that shaped the public's perception of how the American justice system worked. The public might not have been able to grasp every nuance of the latest Supreme Court decision, but they could sit and marvel when, for example, against overwhelming odds, Clarence Darrow secured a 1927 acquittal for Ossian Sweet, a black man accused of murder after defending his Detroit home against a white mob. This was life in the raw, and until the advent of radio and the movies the headline-making trial was the greatest entertainment in town. Trials were quick, turnover was high, and reporters churned out thousands of words daily to satisfy the public's insatiable appetite for sensation and scandal.

Nowadays, of course, trials may last half a year and be televised. Much of the blame, or credit (depending on the point of view), for this dramatic increase in duration can be laid at the door of expert witnesses. As the laboratory has become ever more advanced and forensically useful, its courtroom importance has soared. This has given rise to what lawyers call the "*CSI* effect," among jurors, an expectation that real life can match the miracles routinely performed each week in the popular TV series. For this reason, both prosecutor and defense want to get in as much science as possible. Because so much of this evidence is highly technical in nature, explaining it to a jury can take a very long time. As the battle lines are drawn, each side will, naturally, attack the opposition's experts as "hired guns." In the second murder trial of famed record producer Phil Spector, who, in 2009, was convicted of murdering Lana Clarkson, the prosecution reacted incredulously to some of the defense testimony. "How does a homicide become suicide? You write a big, fat check," Deputy District Attorney Alan Jackson thundered to the jury. "If you can't change the science, you buy the scientist."[6] (One defense expert was reputedly paid $181,000 for his testimony.) In response, defense attorney Doron Weinberg took dead aim

Phil Spector looks at the jury as they depart the courtroom in March 2009. Spector was later convicted of murdering actress Lana Clarkson. *AP Photo/Al Seib, Pool*

at "lazy county criminalists," who had attempted to fit the facts to suit the government's case. "Crime-lab investigators work with the Sheriff's Department," Weinberg said. "They are a team, and this influences the opinions and the judgments they make. It's not dishonesty but it's bias—institutional bias."[7]

There is nothing particularly novel about either form of attack, attorneys have been using them ever since the birth of professional witnesses in the 19th century; the only difference is that, thanks to TV, the general public is today far more savvy about such tactics. Just recently, many in the judicial system have even begun to question the wisdom of the "expert witness for hire" as it currently operates. Does it aid or hinder the search for justice? Only time will tell how this argument pans out. One thing is certain; the American judicial procedure has never stood still. It has constantly adjusted to and reflected contemporary times; it has produced more "Trials of the Century" than most people can remember; it has produced verdicts that baffle and verdicts that make the blood run cold; and it has also produced some of the most dramatic and sensational stories in the nation's history.

The Arrest

An arrest is the act of placing a person in custody or under restraint, usually following the commission of a crime. Since depriving a person of his or her liberty is a serious matter, the law goes to great lengths to provide safeguards designed to protect the rights of the individual. First and foremost among these is the question of legality: Is there probable cause to arrest someone? If so, has the arrest warrant been properly actioned, or in other words, authorized and carried out? Get it wrong and the fallout can be calamitous. For instance, any evidence discovered from an illegally authorized warrant could be thrown out of court on grounds that the search is unlawful. This is the so-called **fruit of the poisoned tree**. In some situations illegal arrest practices may even render a confession of the defendant inadmissible at the trial.

Such examples make it clear that the arrest procedure is a legal minefield through which even the most experienced law enforcement officers tread warily. Until recent times, most of what happened between arrest and arraignment was often shrouded in mystery. There was a good reason for this; in some jurisdictions unscrupulous police officers resorted to the "third degree"—a systematic beating of suspects—as a routine method of loosening tongues and producing confessions. Newspaper readers became used to photographs of suspects, their heavily bruised faces bearing the all-too-obvious effects of jailhouse brutality. Nowadays, the video cameras are whirring constantly—or they certainly should be—during all police interviews, a practice that has notably reduced the level of abuse. Of course, there will always be the occasional rotten apple in any investigative unit, but, for the most part, the rights of the arrested prisoner in custody have never been better protected. Much of the credit for this improvement can be directly attributed to a case that occurred in Arizona in the early 1960s. There was nothing about the circumstances to suggest that here was a case destined to make legal history—the details, though hideously traumatic for the victim, were depressingly commonplace—but what happened in the Phoenix jailhouse in March 1963 would reverberate around the United States and change the face of American justice forever.

Just before midnight on March 2, 1963, an 18-year-old concession stand attendant left the Paramount Theatre in downtown Phoenix where she worked and caught the bus home. After alighting from the bus she was accosted by a stranger who dragged her into the rear seat of his car. Pressing something sharp to the terrified woman's neck—she feared it was a knife, but the attacker later claimed it was a nail file—he tied her hands and feet and drove off. Twenty minutes later, when they were in the desert, he braked to a halt and climbed into the backseat. Although the young woman fought and screamed she was helpless in the face of her attacker's advances. "I was trying to get away," she testified later, "but he was a lot stronger than I was, and I couldn't do anything."[1]

Later that night, the attacker dropped his victim off near her home. She was disheveled and terrified. A family member immediately called the police. The woman described her attacker as a bespectacled Mexican, late 20s, wearing a white T-shirt and blue jeans, and driving an old, light-colored, four-door sedan, possibly a Ford or Chevrolet. Because of some slight inconsistencies in her story, the police were less than diligent in pursuing any suspect. But quite by chance, one week later the woman and her brother-in-law were in downtown Phoenix when they spotted a parked car that she said closely resembled the vehicle used in the attack. The brother-in-law, a car buff, recognized it as a 1953 Packard. As they drew nearer, the driver abruptly sped off. The brother-in-law made a mental note of the license plate—DFL-312—and rushed to phone the police. Records showed that the license plate DFL-312 was registered to a late model Oldsmobile, but the brother-in-law insisted that the car he had seen was a Packard. A check of similar numbers revealed that DFL-317 *was* a Packard, registered to a Twila N. Hoffman. Further inquiries showed that Hoffman's common-law husband, Ernesto Arturo Miranda, age 23, fit the attacker's description almost exactly. Miranda had a long history of erratic and criminal behavior; this included arrests for robbery, and convictions for burglary, auto theft, and assault with intent to rape.

On March 13, 1963, Miranda was apprehended at his home at 2525 West Maricopa and taken to police headquarters in Phoenix. There, two officers, Carroll Cooley and Wilfred Young, began grilling him about the attack on the young woman. As Miranda loudly protested his innocence, Cooley and Young turned the screws. They told Miranda he was also the prime suspect in several other attacks on women that had occurred recently in Phoenix, allegations that he vehemently denied. With the interview degenerating into a stalemate, the officers switched tactics. They asked Miranda if he minded taking part in lineup. He agreed on the proviso that he be allowed to go home if he were not identified. The officers said this was fine. Miranda was then placed in a lineup with three other Mexican Americans of similar height and build, though none wore glasses. The victim studied the men through a two-way mirror. Although she did not positively identify Miranda—it had been very dark in the car—she thought that he bore the closest resemblance to her attacker. Cooley and Young then reinterviewed Miranda. He was told, falsely, that he had been identified, and did he want to make a statement. Miranda thought for a moment, then nodded his head. Two hours later he signed a written confession that began, "I, Ernest A. Miranda [*sic*], do hereby swear that I make this statement voluntarily and of my own free will, with no threats, coercion, or promises of immunity, and with full knowledge of my legal rights, understanding any statement I make may be used against me." He added, "I . . . am 23 years of age and have completed the 8th grade in school."

When Miranda had finished the confession, the victim was brought to the room where he was being held. She stood in the doorway. Although she had failed to positively identify him, Miranda now turned to the police officers present and admitted that she was the woman he had attacked. It was a kind of identification in reverse. (Significantly, as soon as the woman heard Miranda speak, she identified his voice as that of her assailant.) During this same statement, Miranda also confessed to eight other crimes, including robbery and attempted rape. With Miranda under lock and key, Cooley and Young now switched their attention to other duties, little realizing the legal firestorm that they had ignited.

Subsequently, Miranda was arraigned at the courthouse on charges of kidnapping and rape. Arraignment is generally the first encounter that an accused person has with the court prior to trial. At arraignment the charges are read and the accused usually enters a plea of guilt or innocence. If he or she chooses not to plead, a plea of not guilty will be entered on their behalf. A guilty plea will usually result in the case being handed over for judgment. Sometimes the court will permit a guilty plea to be withdrawn. At this time, Miranda entered a plea of not guilty.

As an indigent, Miranda was granted a court-appointed defender. When Alvin Moore studied the evidence against his client he did so with a strong sense of foreboding. Thanks to Miranda's confession, the state's case looked ironclad. And yet there was something about the confession that troubled Moore. He had worked in the law for almost 50 years and he was under no illusions about some of the often underhanded methods officers used to extract confessions. This confession, he felt sure, had been obtained improperly, and he intended to move for its inadmissibility.

First, though, Moore had to overcome another legal headache. Miranda had also been charged with having attacked and robbed another woman on November 27, 1962, and the state wanted to try the two cases simultaneously. The court agreed. However, one day before the intended trial date, Moore filed a notice of intention to prove that his client was insane at the time of the attacks and was insane now, making him unfit to plead. This put everything on hold until Miranda could be examined by two psychiatrists. Although Miranda was found to be mentally competent, the court now reversed its earlier decision and agreed to Moore's request that the cases be tried separately.

The trial got underway on June 20, 1963. Much of the early testimony centered on defense claims that the victim had not done enough to resist her assailant—under Arizona law at the time, anything less than virtually fighting until one's last breath was regarded as com-pliance on the part of the victim—and, therefore, there was no case for Miranda to answer. In a case of this kind, attacks on the victim's character and credibility are a recognized defense strategy, however distasteful they might appear. On this occasion, Moore was unsuc-cessful in his attempts to blacken the victim's name and reputation.

THE RIGHT TO SILENCE

An accused person has hard-won rights enshrined in the Constitution and chief among these is the absolute right to silence. At no time is the defendant required to prove his or her innocence. It is the state or the federal government that has originated this action, and the burden of proof lies entirely with them. For this reason, the defendant cannot be legally compelled to say a word. Nor is the court allowed to comment if the defendant chooses to exercise this right. It wasn't always thus.

Before 1965, a provision in the California state constitution explicitly granted prosecutors the power to ask the jury to draw an inference of guilt if a defendant refused to testify in his own defense. This was challenged in *Griffin v. California,* 380 U.S. 609. In 1965, the Supreme Court ruled, by a 6-2 major-ity, that this provision violated the Self-Incrimination Clause of the Fifth Amendment of the Federal Constitution. Henceforth, California courts were forbidden to comment if a defendant declined to take the stand.

In higher-profile cases, it has become increasingly com-mon for defendants to exercise this right to silence. This can be a double-edged sword. In the eyes of the law, silence is not supposed to jeopardize a defendant's chances with a jury. But juries are as varied as the crimes they try. Some will view a defendant's refusal to take the stand with grave suspicion; oth-ers will set aside prejudice and concentrate on the evidence. This latter reaction is how it should be, but in many trials the verdict of the jury is dictated as much by emotion as the law.

But the canny lawyer was only preparing the ground for what would be his most devastating attack. It came during his cross-examination of Cooley.

"Officer Cooley, in the taking of this statement, what did you say to the defendant to get him to make this statement?"

"I asked the defendant if he would . . . write the same story that he just told me, and he said that he would."

"Did you warn him of his rights?"

"Yes, sir, at the heading of the statement is a paragraph typed out, and I read this paragraph to him out loud."[2]

Later in the exchange with Cooley, Moore sharpened his focus. "I don't see in the statement that it says where he is entitled to the advice of an attorney before he made it."

"No, sir," replied Cooley.

"Is it not your practice to advise people you arrest that they are entitled to the services of an attorney before they make a statement?"

"No, sir."[3]

At this point, Moore turned to Judge Yale McFate and objected to the confession being admitted as evidence, on the grounds that Miranda's Fifth Amendment rights had been infringed. Judge McFate was having none of it. As the law then stood, constitutional protection under the Fifth Amendment was thought to stop at the jailhouse door. Under this interpretation, McFate ruled that the confession could be admitted. With his objection overruled, Moore had nowhere to turn. The confession was deadly. On June 27, 1963, after five hours of deliberation, the jury convicted Miranda and he was sentenced to two concurrent terms of 20 to 30 years imprisonment.

Ordinarily this would have been the end of the story, but Moore was incensed by what he felt to be the injustice suffered by Miranda, and he appealed the case to the Arizona Supreme Court. On April 22, 1965, the court unanimously rejected the appeal, saying:

The facts and circumstances in the instant case show that the statement was voluntary, made by defendant of his own free will, that no threats or use of force or coercion or promise of immunity were made; and that he understood his legal right and the statement might be used against him . . .

notwithstanding the fact that he did not have an attorney at the time he made the statement . . . [the] defendant's constitutional rights were not violated, and it was proper to admit the statement in evidence.[4]

By now, though, the Miranda case had become headline news among scholars of constitutional law. And when it was announced that the United States Supreme Court would consider the case, Moore, in his mid-70s and not in the best of health, graciously stepped aside, clearing the way for attorneys John Flynn and John P. Frank to take over. They appeared before the Supreme Court on February 28, 1966. Everything, they said, hinged on the following argument: that the Arizona court had been wrong in deciding that Miranda, a man of limited intelligence, should have been sufficiently aware of his Fifth Amendment rights without having them spelled out by the officers.

It was a compelling argument and one that worked. On June 13, 1966, Chief Justice Earl Warren, speaking for a 5 to 4 majority, reversed Miranda's conviction because it was clear that he was not in any way apprised of his right to consult with an attorney and to have one present during the interrogation, nor was his right not to be compelled to incriminate himself effectively protected in any other manner. Without these warnings the statements were inadmissible. The mere fact that he signed a statement which contained a typed-in clause stating that he had "full knowledge" of his "legal rights" did not approach the knowing and intelligent waiver required to relinquish constitutional rights.

For the first time in the United States, clear and unequivocal guidelines had been established about what is and what is not permissible in the interrogation room. It was an overwhelming victory for civil rights and a terrible humiliation for the Arizona judicial system. Without Miranda's discredited confession, the case against him looked to have vaporized into thin air. Some even wondered if the state would bother staging a retrial. And then help arrived from an unexpected quarter—Miranda himself.

While he had been in prison, his relationship with Twila Hoffman had broken down. Miranda, confident that he would soon be freed, had begun a battle with Ms. Hoffman over custody of their daughter. As

(continues on page 32)

THE GIDEON DECISION

The case of Ernesto Miranda might be the most famous example of the Supreme Court acting to protect a defendant's rights, but it is far from being unique. Another of the court's landmark decisions had its genesis in the early hours of June 3, 1961, when a poolroom in Panama City, Florida, was broken into and robbed. A 51-year-old drifter, Clarence Gideon, was arrested and charged with the crime. Two months later he went on trial. As the law then stood, Gideon, although indigent, was not automatically entitled to the services of a court-appointed defense lawyer. A 1942 Supreme Court decision, *Betts v. Brady*, 316 U.S. 455, stated that responsibility for deciding this lay with the individual states; only where a defendant was facing a federal charge was the right extended automatically. Although many states did exceed the statutory requirement and provide all felony defendants with counsel, Florida did not. This meant that Gideon was on his own. He did his best to defend himself against some highly dubious eyewitness testimony, but he was hopelessly outgunned by the state prosecutor. At the end of a trial that lasted just one day, he was convicted and imprisoned for five years.

Gideon refused to let the matter lie.

Outraged by the verdict, and more especially by the way he had been abandoned by the judicial system, he appealed to the Florida Supreme Court. They turned him down. He then wrote a five-page document to the United State Supreme Court. Against all odds, they agreed to hear his appeal. Oral argument took place on January 14, 1963, and this time Gideon had the benefit of excellent counsel, Abe Fortas, who, two years later, would himself be appointed to the Supreme Court. He cited the case of Clarence Darrow, one of America's finest attorneys who, when he faced accusations of bribing a juror, was smart enough to realize that he needed the services of a lawyer. It was time, said Fortas, for the law to change. The court agreed. On March 18, 1963, it unanimously overruled *Betts v. Brady*, saying that all felony defendants were entitled to legal representation, irrespective of the crime charged. Justice Hugo L. Black wrote the opinion that set aside Gideon's conviction:

. . . reason and reflection requires us to recognize that in our adversary system of criminal justice, any person haled into court, who is too poor to hire a lawyer, cannot be assured a fair trial unless counsel is provided for him. This seems to us to be an obvious truth.[5]

Florida, smarting from the humiliation, brought in some big prosecutorial guns for Gideon's retrial but to no avail. This time around, a highly experienced criminal lawyer, W. Fred Turner, was in charge of the defense, and he utterly destroyed the eyewitness testimony against his client. After just one hour of deliberation, the jury acquitted Clarence Gideon of all charges and he was set free. He died in 1972 at age 61.

Clarence Earl Gideon changed the course of legal history when the Supreme Court ruled in his favor, stating that anyone accused of a crime should be guaranteed the right to an attorney, whether or not he or she can afford one. *AP Photo*

(continued from page 29)

emotions neared boiling point, Ms. Hoffman dropped a bombshell—she approached the authorities with details of a conversation she'd had with Miranda shortly after his arrest. During this conversation, she said, Miranda had admitted the rape.

Prosecutors were excited but wary. At issue was the question of whether a common-law wife could testify against her husband. It was even thought possible that the Supreme Court might once again intervene. But in the end, Arizona decided that Ms. Hoffman's testimony was admissible and there was no objection by any superior court. On March 1, 1967, Miranda was once again found guilty and sentenced to a 20- to 30-year prison term.

As a result of this landmark case, the so-called Miranda Warning—a clarification of someone's legal rights before they are taken into custody—quickly became part of the fabric of crime fighting in America and an essential ingredient in hundreds of TV programs and movies. Although the actual wording of the warning varies from one jurisdiction to another, the following is a typical example:

> You have the right to remain silent. If you give up the right to remain silent, anything you say can and will be used against you in a court of law. You have the right to an attorney. If you desire an attorney and cannot afford one, an attorney will be appointed for you before police questioning.

It is important to remember that being advised of the Miranda Warning is not enough; a suspect must specifically waive his or her rights before questioning can commence without the presence of a lawyer. The Supreme Court's action was far from universally popular. In his 1968 presidential campaign, Richard Nixon deplored the Miranda Decision, saying that the Supreme Court was more concerned with safeguarding criminals rather than law-abiding citizens. Since that time, despite antagonism from the highest quarters, the Miranda Decision has withstood all attempts to overturn it and is now standard operating procedure in every police department in the country.

The Supreme Court is the highest judicial body in the United States. Its rulings are not subject to review by another court. *AP Photo/J. Scott Applewhite*

The man at the center of this groundbreaking decision, Ernesto Miranda, was paroled in December 1972. After a lackluster attempt at going straight, he soon drifted back into his old ways. On January 31, 1976, he became embroiled in a card game in a Phoenix bar. Tempers ran high and a fight broke out. During the struggle, Miranda was stabbed to death. His killer fled and was never caught, but another man was held in custody. Before taking him to the police station, the arresting officers read the man his rights. In police jargon, the suspected had been "Mirandized."

3

The Prosecution

Assessing whether to prosecute someone on a criminal charge is a decision not taken lightly. There has to be—or there ought to be—sufficient evidence to convince a jury beyond a reasonable doubt that the defendant is guilty of the crime charged. This sounds simple enough, but it is an area fraught with difficulties. Not all cases are clear-cut, and it is the job of the prosecutor to sift through the evidence and to decide whether legal action is appropriate. Because trials are prohibitively expensive, no prosecutor wants to gain a reputation for bringing frivolous actions if there isn't the reasonable expectation of a conviction. This is why district attorneys' offices tend to trumpet their conviction rates—anything in the 90 percent plus range is considered good—and downplay the actual crime-solving rate, which is often dramatically lower. They know that a high-profile acquittal is a guaranteed vote loser come election time.

Setting aside the political element, which rarely strays far from any prosecutor's mind, it is then a question of prioritizing. Just how strong is this particular case? Move higher up the serious crime ladder, and the bigger the stakes become. This is especially true in homicide cases. Often everything hinges on the perceived level of malevolent intent. Did the prisoner really mean to kill the victim? Or was this death the result of a struggle that went tragically wrong? Maybe it was self-defense or just a straightforward tragic accident? These are the kinds of scenarios that the prosecutor has to consider. Find enough gray areas and things start sliding into the often murky realm of the plea bargain, and all the behind-the-scenes legal horse-trading that goes with it.

But there are other issues. America has two distinct codes of justice. One operates at the state level; the other is federal. The overwhelming majority of criminal trials are dealt with at the state level. Generally, federal jurisdiction is called into play only when crimes are committed on federal property; when the victims of crimes happen to be federal employees; or in certain specific crimes. Kidnapping, for instance, was made a federal offense in 1932, following the abduction of Charles Lindbergh Jr., the 20-month-old son of the world-famous aviator.

Mostly, the state and federal prosecutors work independently of each other, and for much of the nation's history the two have tended to keep out of each other's way. But in the 1960s the rules of the game began to change. The bitterly divisive struggle for African-American civil rights in the South, was threatening to make a mockery of the state justice system. For an angry federal government in Washington, D.C., this was an intolerable situation—one that could not be allowed to continue.

On the morning of June 21, 1964, two civil rights campaigners, Michael Schwerner, 24, and James Chaney, 21, left Meridian in east central Mississippi in a blue Ford station wagon. They were members of the Congress of Racial Equality (CORE). With them was Andrew Goodman, 20, an **anthropology** major who had arrived from New York the previous day. It was a hot, steamy southern day, with the temperature climbing into the mid-90s, as they headed for neighboring Neshoba County. Their destination was the small town of Longdale, where, just a few days earlier, a Black-attended church had been burned. They wanted to see for themselves how much damage had been inflicted. All three men knew the risks they were taking as they entered Neshoba County; this was dangerous territory for northern liberals. Aware that their presence was sure to arouse local hostility, they had left details of their itinerary with friends.

Their concerns were justified. That afternoon the trio was pulled over for speeding, just outside the small town of Philadelphia, by local sheriff's deputy, Cecil Price. According to Price, the car was traveling at more than twice the speed limit in a 30 mph zone. Chaney, an African American, was at the wheel, but Price also decided to arrest Schwerner and Goodman, both Jewish. All three men were taken into custody and held, **incommunicado**, for several hours. They were not mistreated in the jailhouse and were even given a meal. At around 10:00 P.M., after paying a $20 fine, they were released. All three got back in their station wagon and drove off into the sweltering night. They then vanished.

Their disappearance rang alarm bells in Washington, D.C. Within 24 hours, President Lyndon Johnson directed the Federal Bureau of Investigation (FBI) to investigate the disappearance. This was unusually fast federal intervention. A government spokesman justified the move by saying, "We are investigating the possibility that they are being held against their will by persons who are not law enforcement officers or that they are otherwise being deprived of their civil liberties."[1] There was also a realization in Washington that Mississippi law enforcement agencies were notoriously lax in investigating civil rights issues. Just one year previously, on June 12, 1963, a prominent black activist named Medgar Evers had been gunned down in the driveway of his home in Jackson, Mississippi. That crime had gone unsolved (until 1994 when Byron De La Beckwith was convicted of Evers' murder). Washington didn't want a repeat of that fiasco.

On June 23, 1964, acting on a tip-off, FBI agents found the burnt-out Ford station wagon in a swamp on Bogue Chitto Creek, just off State Highway 21, about 15 miles northeast of Philadelphia. There was no sign of the missing men. This discovery was the cue for a huge influx of federal agents to the area. They weren't expecting a warm welcome, but the level of hostility and obstructive behavior that greeted them was astonishing. Neshoba County was a hotbed of Ku Klux Klan (KKK) activity, and suddenly everyone appeared to have developed a bad case of amnesia or temporary blindness. But the agents wouldn't be thwarted. They chipped away at the resistance and gradually tongues started to loosen, especially when the FBI started cutting hefty checks in return for information, or so it was later alleged.

The breakthrough came on August 4. Forty-four days after they had disappeared, the bodies of Schwerner, Chaney, and Goodman were recovered from beneath a newly erected earthen dam, about six miles southwest of Philadelphia, and about 20 miles from where the car had been found. They had been buried so deeply that it took a mechanical

MISSING

CALL FBI

THE FBI IS SEEKING INFORMATION CONCERNING THE DISAPPEARANCE AT PHILADELPHIA, MISSISSIPPI, OF THESE THREE INDIVIDUALS ON JUNE 21, 1964. EXTENSIVE INVESTIGATION IS BEING CONDUCTED TO LOCATE GOODMAN, CHANEY, AND SCHWERNER, WHO ARE DESCRIBED AS FOLLOWS:

ANDREW GOODMAN   **JAMES EARL CHANEY**   **MICHAEL HENRY SCHWERNER**

RACE:	White	Negro	White
SEX:	Male	Male	Male
DOB:	November 23, 1943	May 30, 1943	November 6, 1939
POB:	New York City	Meridian, Mississippi	New York City
AGE:	20 years	21 years	24 years
HEIGHT:	5'10"	5'7"	5'9" to 5'10"
WEIGHT:	150 pounds	135 to 140 pounds	170 to 180 pounds
HAIR:	Dark brown; wavy	Black	Brown
EYES:	Brown	Brown	Light blue
TEETH:		Good: none missing	
SCARS AND MARKS:		1 inch cut scar 2 inches above left ear.	Pock mark center of forehead, slight scar on bridge of nose, appendectomy scar, broken leg scar.

SHOULD YOU HAVE OR IN THE FUTURE RECEIVE ANY INFORMATION CONCERNING THE WHEREABOUTS OF THESE INDIVIDUALS, YOU ARE REQUESTED TO NOTIFY ME OR THE NEAREST OFFICE OF THE FBI. TELEPHONE NUMBER IS LISTED BELOW.

DIRECTOR
FEDERAL BUREAU OF INVESTIGATION
UNITED STATES DEPARTMENT OF JUSTICE
WASHINGTON, D. C. 20535
TELEPHONE, NATIONAL 8-7117

June 29, 1964

FBI/DOJ

The FBI released this poster seeking information about the whereabouts of murdered civil rights activists Andrew Goodman, James Earl Chaney, and Michael Henry Schwerner in June 1964. *MPI/Getty Images* digger to find them. Autopsies showed that all three men had been shot to death. Schwerner died from a single bullet, as did Goodman. Chaney was shot three times.

By now investigators were pretty sure they had pieced together the murderous events of June 21. An informant within the KKK had not only led them to the bodies, but also claimed that Price had been the architect of the crime. It had been Price who'd contacted other KKK members, and had given them time to organize a lynch mob. When Price freed the men at 10:00 P.M., he had then tailed them in his car and stopped them once again. This time he delivered the men into the hands of his co-conspirators.

Names of the gang members being bandied about included that of Sam Bowers, said to be the chief of the ultra-secretive White Knights, a militant wing of the Ku Klux Klan; Olen Burrage, on whose land the bodies were found; and Edgar Ray "Preacher" Killen, a fundamentalist minister and sawmill operator. By the time the dust settled, agents were confident they could file charges against 19 suspects. But did they have enough to get convictions? It turned out that they couldn't even get the cases into court. On September 30, after a local inquiry of mind-numbing slowness, a Neshoba County grand jury failed to return indictments against a single suspect.

For Washington this was the final humiliating straw. Twice that year it had sat helplessly on the sidelines and fumed as all-white Mississippi juries deadlocked over the guilt of Byron De La Beckwith, the accused killer of Medgar Evers. White supremacists were literally laughing their way out of local courtrooms, safe in the knowledge that no jury would dare convict them of murder. There had to be another way to provide justice for Schwerner, Chaney, and Goodman.

The solution came in an 1870 civil rights statute. It simply stated that everyone had the constitutional right to live. Federal attorneys interpreted this to mean that the 19 suspects could be charged with conspiring "under color of the laws of Mississippi" to violate the rights of the three by depriving them of "life or liberty without due process of law."[2] If convicted they faced a maximum punishment of 10 years and $5,000 fine.

Despite furious accusations by Mississippi that this amounted to unwarranted federal interference in what was a state crime, in 1965 the government succeeded in obtaining indictments against 18 of the accused (Bowers was not included at this time). But United States District Judge W. Harold Cox invalidated the indictments in a decision saying that the selection of federal juries did not represent a cross-section of citizens. Subsequently, jury selection methods were changed to provide wider representation, and on February 28, 1967, 19 fresh indictments—including Bowers—were handed down.

With such an immense amount riding on this trial, the prosecution was entrusted to John Doar, head of the Justice Department's civil rights division. Doar had a strong track record. In October 1962, he had shepherded Black student James Meredith through his riot-torn admission to the University of Mississippi. Confronting frenzied mobs, dodging stones and bricks, and learning to stand impassively by while every kind of vile epithet was hurled at him became a way of life. During his time at the Department of Justice, Doar prosecuted more than 30 voting rights cases, but nothing could approach the tension or the importance of this trial in Meridian, Mississippi.

After three years of stonewalling, hedging, and blatant obstructionism, the trial finally opened on October 7, 1967. The atmosphere was heavily charged. Across from the courthouse, a parked pickup truck belonging to one of the defendants proudly displayed a Confederate flag from a pole. Crowds gathered to cheer the defendants as they entered the courthouse. Inside the courtroom, the prosecution team, led by John Doar, looked positively skimpy when arrayed against no fewer than a dozen defense attorneys, and picking a jury was a hard-fought contest. After two days, that saw every prospective Black juror rejected, an all-white jury of seven women and five men was impaneled. From the outset it became clear that the defense lawyers felt they had an ally in trial judge Cox. In the past his civil rights record had been questionable. Bowers knew this. When the bodies were discovered, he had smirked that "Judge Cox would probably make them take those bodies and put them back,"[3] because they were found on an illegal search. But on this occasion, with the media microscope on full power, Judge Cox dealt a crushing blow to those expectations, dismissing out-of-hand a slew of frivolous defense objections. It was time to get on with the evidence.

One of the first prosecution witnesses was FBI agent Jay Cochran Jr. Although he claimed not to know how the FBI had obtained the information that led to the bodies, he did describe how the bodies had been found. He had gone to the site with heavy earth-moving equipment, he said, after spotting it from a helicopter. Over defense protests, photos of

THE PLEA BARGAIN

One of the most important decisions that any prosecutor has to make is whether to offer the prisoner a plea bargain, which is a kind of legal deal by which the defendant pleads guilty to a specific charge or lesser charge in exchange for a lighter sentence. Viewed as a pragmatic necessity by some, and reprehensible by others, the practice of plea bargaining is an integral component of the American judicial system. Without it the courts would simply grind to a halt. Indeed, the vast majority of cases are settled by plea bargains rather than by criminal trials. Think of it as a kind of fast-track through what is otherwise a gridlocked legal maze.

America certainly needs it.

According to the FBI in 2008, there were 22,299,954 serious crimes in the United States.[4] Only a minuscule fraction of these offenses will ever result in an arrest and trial, but every arm of the judicial process knows that a tiny percentage of criminals are responsible for the vast majority of crimes. Lock up these bad guys and the public can sleep a little easier, or so the reasoning goes. For example, say a known burglar is arrested for a particular break in, and there is evidence to suggest that he has been responsible for a string of similar crimes in the same neighborhood. Overworked prosecutors will make it clear to the prisoner that the courts will go easier on him if he pleads guilty to all the offenses, rather than tie up the court's time in fighting every charge individually. The prisoner agrees. He gets a lighter sentence and the courts can the dead men were shown to the jury. Not that this seemed to greatly trouble the defendants. Boredom had been the default attitude since their trial began.

Much of the government's case was based on the word of informants and turncoats. Prosecutor Doar admitted quite candidly that the FBI "had to pay money for information leading to the solution of the case."[5] One of those on the government payroll was a Meridian

---

move on. It might not be ideal, but it does keep the wheels of justice moving—just.

Plea bargaining operates across the criminal spectrum, from straightforward robbery to homicide, but it comes under the most scrutiny—and receives the most criticism—in higher-profile cases. This is where the prosecutor is really tested. For instance, the state might be convinced that the prisoner is a heartless murderer, but if the evidence is weak, rather than pursue a death penalty conviction that might backfire and let a killer walk free, the prosecutor decides to offer the defendant a deal: plead guilty to second-degree murder and the prosecution will take the death penalty off the table; the defendant is then looking at a maximum of life imprisonment with a possibility of parole down the road. Depending on the prisoner's anxiety levels—and ego—most will grab the offer with both hands. Both sides benefit; the taxpayer has been spared the expense of a costly trial and the prisoner avoids a date with the executioner.

There are many critics, though, who question the ethics of the plea bargain system, arguing that it undermines the constitutional right to trial by jury. This is not a view endorsed by the United States Supreme Court. In *Santobello v. New York,* 404 U.S. 257, 261 (1971), the Court wrote that "plea bargains are important in the administration of justice both at the state and at the federal levels . . . [and] serve an important role in the disposition of today's heavy calendars." In an ideal world plea bargains wouldn't exist. For now, they are as fundamental to the judicial system as juries.

policeman, Sergeant Carlton Miller, 43, who testified that he joined the KKK in March/April 1964 and became a paid FBI informer the following September. He named several of the defendants as active KKK members and recalled being told, one week after their disappearance, that Chaney, Goodman, and Schwerner were "buried 15 feet in a dam."[6] In chilling detail, Miller spelled out the KKK's protocols, used to determine which victims deserved "whipping, beatings" and which were earmarked for "elimination."[7]

Another disaffected Klansman, James Jordan, a 40-year-old construction worker, was accompanied into the courthouse by five armed guards. Since becoming an informant in 1964, Jordan had been holed-up in Florida and Georgia for his own safety. The pressure clearly got to him. At one stage in court he collapsed and had to be given medical treatment. What he had to say, though, was damning. Under the contemptuous gaze of the defendants, he told of being posted as a lookout down a country lane, a short distance from where the three men were being held. "I heard car doors slam, some loud talk that I could not distinguish, and then I heard several shots."[8] He later saw the three bodies dumped into a prepared grave that was then bulldozed over.

When Delmar Dennis, another renegade Klansman, took the stand, the defendants looked on in open-mouthed disbelief. At no time had they ever suspected that this 27-year-old minister and high-ranking KKK official was also an FBI informant. Dennis testified that Bowers bragged to other Klan members of his involvement in the Neshoba killings, crowing, "It was the first time that Christians had planned and carried out the execution of a Jew."[9] Dennis confirmed that, prior to the killings, it had been announced to a Klan meeting that Bowers had ordered the "elimination"[10] of Schwerner. Asked by Doar what Bowers meant by elimination, Dennis replied, "He meant killing a person."[11]

Earlier defense miscalculations about the mood of the court were now compounded when defense attorney Laurel Weir, cross-examining a prosecution witness, the Reverend Charles Johnson, asked if it was true that he [Johnson] and Schwerner had tried to "get young Negro males to sign statements that they would rape one white woman a week during the hot summer of 1964 here in Mississippi."[12] Judge Cox interrupted sharply. After a lengthy and volatile exchange, the judge declared, "I'm not going to allow a farce to be made of this trial and everybody might as well get that through their heads, including every one of the defendants."[13]

YOU CAN'T SIT THERE!

Not all battles in the fight for civil rights revolved around murders and lynchings. Other, equally important, campaigns were waged. In 1958 Bruce Boynton, a black student at Howard University Law School in Washington, D.C., took a Trailways bus from Washington to his home in Montgomery, Alabama. On a 45-minute layover at the Trailways bus terminal in Richmond, Virginia, the passengers went inside to eat. Boynton entered the segregated restaurant, sat in the white section and ordered a sandwich and tea. When asked to move to the colored section he refused, saying that as an interstate passenger he was protected by federal antisegregation laws. Declining to leave, he was arrested by local police, charged with trespass, and fined $10.

When lawyers for the National Association for the Advancement of Colored People (NAACP) appealed the judgment, the state of Virginia found that Boynton had no such federal protection and upheld the original sentence.

In 1960 *Boynton v. Virginia* found its way to the Supreme Court. On December 5, 1960, the court decided 7 to 2 in favor of Boynton, the first time since 1946 it had divided on a matter of racial segregation. A strong factor in the Court's decision was the testimony of the restaurant manager that, although local residents did use the restaurant, most of the establishment's business derived from Trailways passengers.

The operators of the restaurant, Bus Terminal Restaurants, Inc., had anticipated the Supreme Court's decision. Earlier it had announced that, as of August 1960, none of their establishments would be racially segregated. For the first time a bridge was built between the federal government and the civil rights movement, as Washington sent a clear message that interstate facilities were for the use of all citizens, irrespective of color.

By now it was clear that the defense had lost its focus and with it their grip on the jury. The claims and counterclaims flew viciously. One of the defendants, Horace Burrage, swore that Jordan, far from being a distant lookout, was actually the person who shot Chaney. And the estranged wife of Delmar Dennis testified that she wouldn't believe a single word her preacher husband said, even if he swore on a stack of Bibles. A string of witnesses came forward to provide dubious and various alibis for the defendants. There were also shameful attacks on the characters of the dead men. Contrast these meddling outsiders, said defense attorney Herman Alford, with the defendants; men he described as "pure as the driven snow. They have been harassed by the Federal Government. Neshoba County is innocent; these defendants are innocent."[14] The defense produced more than 40 character witnesses, among them, Amie Coleman, a Black woman who had worked for seven years in Bowers' movie house. "He's a very nice person,"[15] she said.

When a Mrs. Finnis McAdory testified that at the estimated time of the killings—around midnight—she and her husband were with Price at the police station in Philadelphia, Doar asked her motivation for taking the stand. After considerable hesitation, she replied that she was "testifying for my county."[16]

Which was precisely the point that Doar emphasized in his closing speech to the jury. "A thousand eyes explored every corner of Neshoba County . . . but Neshoba County closed ranks and remained silent. . . . Rarely in the history of law enforcement was information so difficult to obtain."[17] Because of this reticence, Washington felt impelled to act. But, he emphasized, such action did not mean that the federal government was "invading Philadelphia or Neshoba County, Mississippi, it means only that these defendants are tried for a crime under Federal law in a Mississippi City, before a Mississippi Federal Judge, in a Mississippi courtroom, assisted by Mississippi courtroom officials before twelve men and women from the state of Mississippi."[18] The sole responsibility for determining the guilt or innocence of the defendants remained "in the hands where it should remain, the hands of twelve citizens from the state of Mississippi."[19]

This was shrewd psychology. Throughout the trial, Doar had wisely avoided turning this case into an indictment of the state; he knew his best chance of victory lay in appealing to sound common sense. The federal government, he said, was merely trying to seek a modicum of justice for three men who had been victims of a "diabolical plot," engineered by Price, using "the machinery of his office—the badge, the car, the jail, the gun . . . ."[20] to further the conspiracy. Answering defense claims that the government had had to resort to paid informants, Doar regretted this expedient, but added that it had been necessary because, as he put it, "Midnight murder in the rural area of Neshoba County provides few witnesses."[21] He continued: "If there is to be any hope for this land of ours, the Federal Government has the duty [to oppose] evil forces that seize control of law enforcement."[22]

Doar's final charge to the jury was a plea for common sense. "If you find them not guilty, it would be as true to say there was no nighttime release by Cecil Price, there are no White Knights, there are no young men dead, there was no murder."[23] He urged them to stand firm.

In response, the defense mustered an unpleasant assortment of slurs and innuendos, centered around the mind-boggling assertion that the three young men had brought this tragedy on themselves and that they had been deliberately sacrificed by the civil rights movement for political advantage. As arguments go, it was snatched from the gutter, and, in the face of so much evidence, it reeked of vindictiveness and nothing else.

After Judge Cox's summing-up, the case went to the jury at 4:24 P.M. on October 18. Cox allowed the jury to go home at night as long as they did not talk to anyone about the case. "If I get the impression you're not following the rules of the court I'm going to keep you all together."[24] Like everyone else, Cox had seen that huge Confederate flag across the street.

After a day's deliberation, the jury declared themselves deadlocked. Judge Cox refused to declare a mistrial and ordered a return to deliberations, reminding them of the expense of another trial and the necessity for them to reach a verdict. The admonishment worked. On October 20 the jury found Price and Bowers and five other defendants guilty. They could reach no verdict against four defendants; the remaining defendants were acquitted. When news of the verdicts filtered out from the courthouse, the crowds seemed dazed. History had been made. For

Escorted by a sheriff's deputy, former Klansman Edgar Ray Killen, charged with the murder of three civil rights campaigners, walks into court in January 2005. Killen later was convicted and sentenced to 60 years in prison. *AP Photo/Neshoba Democrat, Kyle Carter, Pool*

the first time a Mississippi jury had convicted white defendants of civil rights violations against Black people or civil rights workers, and this in a state where a series of racial outrages had gone unpunished since the 1955 murder of 15-year-old Emmett Till.

Announcing himself in complete agreement with the verdicts, Judge Cox set December 29 as sentencing day. At that time he imposed a 10-year jail term on Bowers, and six years for Price. The other convicted men received sentences varying from three to 10 years.

Edgar Ray Killen, one of those freed on a hung jury, did not escape justice forever. New evidence emerged that it was he who had recruited the lynch mob, and on June 21, 2005, the 41st anniversary of the crime, Killen, by now 80 years old, was convicted of triple manslaughter and sentenced to 60 years imprisonment.

Bowers' troubles continued to mount. In August 1998 he was convicted, at the third time of asking, of the murder of Vernon Dahmer, a black activist who died when his Hattiesburg, Mississippi, home was firebombed on January 10, 1966. Bowers' life sentence proved to be just that. He died in the state penitentiary on November 5, 2006, of cardiac arrest, at age 82.

At one time federal intervention in criminal matters was a rarely used tool. It is now more common, with most interventions being inspired by racially motivated crimes. When, in 1992, four Los Angeles Police Department officers were acquitted of using excessive force in the arrest of Rodney King—an arrest that had been captured on videotape—the resulting riots in Los Angeles left 53 dead, thousands injured, and more than $1 billion in financial losses. One year later, the four officers were back in court, this time on federal charges of having violated King's civil rights. Two officers were convicted and sentenced to 30 months, the others were acquitted. For many, this second trial flouted the constitutional protection against double jeopardy, and owed more to a public desire for vengeance rather than a quest for justice. Having two bites at the legal cherry might soothe ruffled consciences, but does it make for good law? The arguments will continue to rage.

The Great
Defender

America has more lawyers than the rest of the world combined. Exact figures are hard to come by, but in 2006 the American Bar Association estimated the number at 1.1 million. Most of these practice civil law and will rarely, if ever, see the inside of a criminal courtroom. For those that do harbor ambitions in criminal practice, the choice is clear: prosecution or defense. The former, by definition, requires the individual to become an employee of the state or federal government, and is often used as a springboard to a political career. The latter is more complex. It, too, can involve cashing a government pay check, courtesy of a position in the public defender's office, but going down the defense route also offers one other option—private practice.

It is this field that has provided many of the greatest and most colorful names in American courtroom history—Clarence Darrow, William J. Fallon, Jake Ehrlich, Sam Liebowitz, Jerry Giesler, F. Lee Bailey, Percy Foreman, Gerry Spence, the list goes on and on. All achieved near legendary status for their ability to win seemingly hopeless cases. Most profited hugely from this talent. (Darrow was an exception, fighting most of his battles in the high-profile but low-paid political arena.) Yet the impression remains that it's the ego-boosting rush that drives them on to snatch victory from the jaws of defeat. There is something about the lone maverick lawyer, taking on the establishment and winning, that resonates in the American psyche. But there is another edge to this sword. Every defense lawyer, at one time or another, has had to suffer the contemptuous sneer that generally accompanies the question: "How on earth can you defend someone you know to be guilty?"

The stock and, some say, glib answer is: "How would I know; I never ask." But this, of course, dodges the issue. Any defense lawyer worth his or her salt will gain some sense of whether or not their client is telling the truth. But it's not their job to judge. They have been trained to provide the best defense possible. Everyone, even the baby-stealing pedophile or the most sadistic serial killer, has the constitutional right to a decent defense and competent counsel. The fact is, sometimes even the blackest case might turn out to be not quite so shadowy as it first appears.

At the end of the 19th century the city of Los Angeles was enjoying the first great boom in its history. The discovery of oil in 1892 had started the rush, triggering an influx of wheeler-dealers, all scrabbling to make their fortunes. One of those who'd prospered more than most was transplanted Texan, Jay E. Hunter. A lawyer by trade, Hunter had grown fat on the madcap real estate and oil markets, and he didn't attempt to hide his success. He was a flashy dresser, prominent in local society and he'd been made a member of the exclusive California Club. He also had a foul temper. In May 1892 he had found himself in court, charged with having smashed a cane on the head of one J. C. Davis, assistant manager of the Juch Opera Company, after the latter had accused him of "not conducting his business as a gentleman, but as a **pettifogger**."[1] The judge reluctantly decided that there was insufficient evidence to go to a jury, and threw out the charges. Hunter was free to continue his bullying ways.

A few years passed and then, in late 1898, he engaged a local handyman named William Alford to repair some plumbing. When Alford presented his bill for $102, Hunter just laughed in his face and refused to pay. Alford kept submitting demands and saw every one rejected. Not even a court judgment could loosen Hunter's notoriously tight purse rings.

Frustrated beyond endurance, and with a pregnant wife and several children to feed, Alford tried a novel tack; he had some flyers printed with the heading *JAY E. HUNTER DOES NOT PAY HIS DEBTS,* and going on to explain the repairs, the court judgment, and Hunter's refusal to pay. On the afternoon of February 18, 1899, at just after four o'clock, Alford, flyers in hand, arrived at Hunter's downtown office in the six-story Stimson building on Spring Street.

The two men met in a fourth-floor corridor. Alford thrust a handbill into the much larger man's face and threatened to start plastering the flyers all over town unless the debt was met immediately. Hunter, brandishing his omnipresent heavy mahogany cane—the silver head alone weighed three pounds—peered down disdainfully at Alford and

PASSING THE BAR

Each year, approximately 40,000 lawyers graduate from America's accredited law schools. But it wasn't always this way. Before the American Revolution, there were no law schools at all in the 13 colonies. Anyone aspiring to the law as a profession had merely to find an attorney willing to take him on as a clerk or apprentice. Admission rules were lax—a sizable bank balance was often the only qualification required for entry—and it was clear that some regulatory tightening up was called for. After the revolution, a few law offices began to specialize in the training of clerks. Out of this grew the first recognized law school, Litchfield School in Connecticut, founded in 1784. Instead of the old mentor/pupil method, for the first time law was taught by means of lectures. This idea proved popular, and before long, colleges that had added law to the general curriculum, adopted the lecture method of teaching. The big breakthrough came in 1817, when Harvard—the oldest university in America—established an independent law school.

Measured against modern standards, the entry criteria remained loose. No previous college experience was necessary, and the basic law school curriculum could be completed in just one year. Not much happened for several decades thereafter, but the second half of the 19th century saw a dramatic surge in the number of law schools, from 15 in 1850 to 102 in 1900. This increase brought with it a more told him to get lost. Tempers began to boil. Other tenants in the building heard the sounds of a heated exchange. And then a shot. Followed by another.

Those first at the scene saw Hunter, blood pumping from a stomach wound, prostrate on the floor, fingers still clutching the cane that had shattered during the scuffle. Above him, gun in hand, stood Alford, frail and bleeding profusely from a head wound. Hunter, who'd been shot twice in the abdomen, was rushed to the California Hospital

rigorous two-year curriculum and exams at the end of the first year.

One of the biggest landmarks in American legal history came on June 9, 1869, when a young Midwestern couple, John and Arabella Mansfield, passed the Iowa state bar exam. Although there was nothing noteworthy about John's success, for Arabella it was a different story. At age 23, she had made history by becoming the first woman attorney in America. Some academics have disputed the claim, pointing out that she never actually attended a law school, but the fact remains that she was the first woman licensed to practice law in the United States. (This didn't exactly open the feminist floodgates. According to the 1890 census, of the 87,422 lawyers nationwide, just 208—or 0.232 percent—were women.)

Arabella Mansfield's achievement demonstrated that, in 1869, it was still possible in some states to bypass law school in pursuit of a legal career, but by the beginning of the 20th century attendance at a law school was an almost universal requirement. (In California it is still possible to sit for the state bar exam without having attended an accredited law school, provided one has participated in an approved course of study in a law office or the chambers of a judge.)

Since 1900, the number of accredited law schools in America has almost doubled, from 102 to 200. The seemingly unstoppable legal conveyor belt produces 70 percent of the world's lawyers; and with another 150,000 students still in the pipeline, it shows no sign of slowing down any time soon.

and operated on immediately. By this time Alford had been disarmed and taken into custody. "I absolutely refuse to discuss the matter,"[2] was his only comment. The following day his predicament, already dire, nose-dived precipitously when Hunter died in the hospital, and Alford found himself facing a charge of first-degree murder. If found guilty he would hang.

The case seemed ironclad. Although there were no witnesses to the shooting, Alford's antipathy toward Hunter was well known, and several people had overheard their quarrel in the corridor. Also, while in the hospital, Hunter had insisted that he had only used the cane to defend himself. Because of the deceased's social prominence, a special prosecutor was appointed to handle the case. Former Senator Stephen M. White was Southern California's premier attorney, massively experienced in criminal trial work and a lethal courtroom performer. With him at the helm, upper-class Los Angelenos could rest easy about the outcome.

Alford, by contrast, had trouble even finding a lawyer. Not only was he almost broke, but his case looked hopeless and the public was baying for blood. But one attorney, Earl Rogers, saw a glimmer of hope and grabbed the case with both hands. At the time of the Alford trial, Rogers was a 29-year-old unknown, with less than two years' courtroom experience behind him. But he was hungry and he was good, very good. In years to come, no less an authority than Clarence Darrow himself, would describe Rogers as "the greatest jury lawyer of his time."[3] Many feel that Rogers practically invented the role of the modern defender. Before Rogers, lawyers relied mainly on rhetoric and theatrics to sway a jury. Rogers had those gifts in abundance, but he brought so much more to the defense table. Nobody studied the background to a case more thoroughly, nobody ferreted out that obscure medical detail better, nobody was better at picking juries, and nobody could touch him in the dubious art of using available tactic to gain an edge. He was, quite simply, brilliant. The only problem was, in 1899, hardly anyone knew this as Roger set about marshaling every ounce of his formidable skills in order to keep Alford's neck out of a noose.

On February 20 Rogers showed up at the funeral home of the Bresee Brothers, where Hunter's body was being prepared for burial. Friends of the deceased did not want an autopsy, but Rogers was insistent. And he

Criminal defense lawyer Clarence Darrow is considered to be one of the greatest trial lawyers to set foot in a courtroom. *AP Photo*

had the coroner at his side. There was no love lost between the Bresee brothers and coroner Lauren T. Holland, especially as Holland wanted the body moved to a favored friend's undertaking business (bodies were highly profitable commodities at the turn of the century and Holland could expect a kickback from his undertaker pal). But Rogers stuck to his guns. The body, he pointed out, was already decomposing, and he demanded an immediate autopsy. Holland agreed and an autopsy was carried out later that same day, together with an inquest. At this hearing, Rogers established that his client would be pleading self-defense. With the formalities out of the way, the following day Hunter's body was shipped back to Austin, Texas. That same morning Alford was arraigned on a charge of murder and held without bail. Inside of a week, though, Rogers had his client back on the streets, having arranged an $8,000 bond.

When the trial opened, Rogers was looking especially debonair. It was typical of the man that he'd spent almost half of his $100 fee on a new suit. With his matinee idol looks and imposing stature, all he needed were the right clothes to cut a dashing figure in court. He was out to make an impression, especially on opposing counsel. Rogers was a former pupil of Stephen M. White's. Now, in his first big case, the newcomer was set to do battle with the lawyer whom everyone called the "little giant."

In court, Rogers listened attentively as Coroner Holland offered his opinion of how Hunter had been shot. Since the bullet had entered Hunter's body above the abdomen and then traveled downward, through the intestines, exiting via the buttocks, he concluded that Alford was standing over his victim when he fired. Rogers managed to soften the impact of Holland's testimony with sarcastic humor, providing the jury with a humorous account of how Holland had fought to gain control of the body in order to line his own pockets. Holland's obvious discomfiture helped deflect attention away from the prisoner.

Rogers made less headway against Dr. C. W. Pierce, a surgeon who had operated on Hunter at the California Hospital. He corroborated Holland's evidence: The bullet had definitely traveled downward through Hunter's body. Such testimony appeared to demolish Alford's claim of self-defense. Yet Rogers wasn't perturbed. He chose not to delve too deeply into this matter at the moment, and, instead, fell back on a recognized tactic of defense lawyers since courts began: Attack the victim.

When F. A. Stephenson, also an attorney in the Stimson building and the first man on the crime scene, took the stand, he, at first, denied all knowledge of Hunter's sadistic track record. But Rogers wouldn't let go. He kept after Stephenson, until the witness finally conceded that, since the tragedy, stories had reached him of Hunter's brutal temper, how he'd beat people about the head with his heavy cane. Every detail of the 1892 incident, when Hunter had narrowly avoided prison for attacking another man, was replayed for the jury. Slowly, Rogers managed to implant in the jury's mind the suggestion that Hunter's cane might have been wielded offensively, not defensively. This was a step in the right direction, but Rogers knew he needed more. White, brilliant on cross-examination, would make Alford jump through hoops if allowed. Rogers searched for a way to neutralize this threat. After several days the solution fell into his lap.

White's legal prowess was the talk of Los Angeles; so was his fondness for bourbon. With each passing trial day, his lunch hour grew longer and more liquid. At first, out of courtesy to White, the judge delayed each afternoon session a few minutes until White arrived. But after a week, with White staggering in almost half an hour late, the judge's patience expired and he took to beginning afternoon proceedings without the "little giant." White's absence threw the burden for much of the prosecution on to Deputy District Attorney Johnstone Jones, a pompous, self-important individual, slow-witted and desperately short of courtroom experience. Known sarcastically as "General," Jones was completely out of his depth and came in for some merciless attorney-baiting at the hands of his eloquent opponent. Rogers didn't miss an opportunity to embarrass Jones, determined to undermine his authority with the jury.

During some medical testimony from Dr. Ralph Hagan, Jones asked where exactly one of the fatal bullets had entered Hunter's body. "On a level with, and four inches from the anterior superior spinous process of the ilium,"[4] was the reply. When Jones asked the witness if he could point out this spot on his [Jones's] body, Rogers leaned over and jabbed his finger into Jones's paunch hard enough to make him grunt. Surprised and gasping for breath, Jones blustered that he hadn't asked Rogers, and "Besides, what do you know about anatomy?"

"He indicated the spot exactly," declared Dr. Hagan.

Rogers smiled innocently at the red-faced prosecutor. "Aren't you going to thank me, General?"[5]

Both judge and jury burst into laughter. What looked like a cheap shot, designed just to raise a laugh and humiliate his opponent, proved to be much more. Rogers had scored a big point; he'd visibly demonstrated his medical knowledge. That would come in handy later.

After several days of testimony the prosecution rested. This conclusion coincided with the noon recess, and Rogers was in a quandary. All he had were a couple of character witnesses, some brief medical testimony, and Alford himself. His entire case would be concluded in one afternoon. By custom, the defendant was the closing witness. This was done out of fairness to the person on trial. If any other witness had varied their testimony or some unexpected damage had been inflicted on the defendant, it allowed the defendant to adjust his or her own evidence to the best advantage. Rogers explained this to Alford, rehearsing his testimony; then he headed for a nearby saloon favored by local attorneys and particularly Senator White. White, already bleary-eyed, called Rogers over and, together, mentor and student enjoyed a convivial drink. The two men discussed the case. White chuckled into his glass and predicted that he would tear Alford's testimony to shreds. He was still guzzling lunch when Rogers, suddenly recalling an important office appointment, announced that he had to leave.

That afternoon at 2 o'clock, when the trial resumed, White was missing as usual. Rogers, in his chair and ready to go, called his first witness—William Alford.

Quickly and without ornamentation, just as Rogers had instructed, Alford told how Hunter had attacked him with the cane, knocked him down, and continued beating him until he feared for his life. Then— and only then—had he drawn his gun from its holster, pointed it up at Hunter, who was bent almost double above him, and pulled the trigger.

After just 15 minutes Rogers spun suddenly toward the prosecution table and barked out his trademark line: "Take the witness!" Jones swallowed hard. The intention had been for White to cross-examine Alford; Jones, unprepared for the task, rose miserably to his feet.

Haltingly and with one eye fixed on the doorway, desperate for White to appear, Jones stumbled into his cross-examination. Alford fielded every question firmly and well, until, urged on by an impatient

THE ORDER TO TESTIFY

An integral feature of the legal system is the *subpoena*. They fall into three main categories. The first, a *subpoena ad testificandum*, more commonly known as a subpoena, literally means to "testify under penalty." It is a formal instrument issued by a court, grand jury, or some other legislative body, commanding the person or organization named in the subpoena to give sworn testimony at a specified time and place about a matter concerned in an investigation or a legal proceeding, such as a trial. A *subpoena duces tecum* commands the recipient to present in court certain evidence, usually documents or papers, necessary to the successful resolution of the controversy. Documentary evidence is, in many respects, considered better than the evidence furnished by witnesses, about which there has always been a certain amount of suspicion (memories can play tricks and there is always the potential for lying). The third form of **subpoena** is the deposition. This means that your sworn testimony will be taken during a phase of the trial process known as discovery, and will likely occur at a lawyer's office.

Subpoenas may be issued by any of the following parties: the judge presiding over the legal proceedings; the clerk of the court where the lawsuit has been filed; an attorney representing one of the parties in the lawsuit; a government lawyer such as the attorney general or district attorney (it should be noted that the government lawyers can issue a subpoena during an investigation, before initiating a legal case).

Given that a subpoena is an order to produce yourself and/or tangible items in a very specific legal setting, it is crucial that it is taken seriously. Failure to comply with a subpoena may lead to a charge of contempt of court, resulting in criminal or civil proceedings.

judge, Jones ran out of steam after just a few minutes and mumbled that he had no further questions.

At that very moment Senator White swayed into the courtroom. He instantly took in the situation, but before he could say a word, Rogers was on his feet, yelling, "No redirect examination," and waving Alford hurriedly from the stand. White, beside himself with rage, said under his breath, "That was a dirty trick, Earl."[6]

Rogers, smiling, resumed his case. He turned to the judge and made an unprecedented request—asking that the intestines of the late Jay Hunter be admitted into evidence. A gasp rattled the courtroom's rafters. White rose unsteadily to his feet, objecting that there was no basis for presenting such unusual evidence. Rogers countered that White himself had provided the basis, by bringing the coroner to the stand and eliciting testimony that Alford's bullet had traveled downward through the intestines. Rogers intended to prove that the shot had actually been fired upward—but he needed the intestines to do it.

Over howls of the prosecution's protest, the judge ruled in Rogers' favor, and for the first time in a California homicide trial, the innards of the deceased were brought into court. Using a colored chart of the intestines, and backed up by the testimony of Dr. Edward Pallete, Rogers presented an alternative and imaginative account of how the bullet came to travel downward through the intestines. It had been caused by Hunter's fury. After shattering his cane on Alford's head, he had then used the splintered fragment as a short club, bending almost double to deliver the blows. Alford, cowering on the ground, had shot up at his assailant, only for the bullet to travel down through Hunter's body while his shoulders were below hip-level, and while his intestines were folded over upon themselves.

It was only a theory, of course, but the jury, dazzled by Rogers's revolutionary charts and technical jargon, gobbled it up and acquitted Alford on grounds of self-defense. Stephen White, the "little giant," limped from court, a broken man, beaten by his own pupil. His reputation never recovered and two years later he was dead.

After the trial there were complaints about the way Rogers had blindsided White, but he fended off all objectors by pointing out that his first duty was to his client. Rogers always knew where his obligations

Legendary defense lawyer Earl Rogers sits at his desk in 1911. A relative unknown on the legal scene at the time, Rogers used his brilliant defense of William Alford in 1898 to launch his career. *Library of Congress*

began and ended. On one occasion, after he successfully defended yet another client on a charge of murder, Rogers had refused to shake the man's hand afterward, snarling, "Get away from me, you slimy pimp. You know you're as guilty as hell!"[7] It is this duality that laypersons find so hard to stomach. What Rogers did wasn't pretty, but it was essential. In time he would go on to become, in the opinion of many, the greatest defense lawyer that America has produced. His range of forensic skills was unrivaled. He was skilled enough in medicine to unsettle any doctor; an expert anatomist; dauntingly knowledgeable about the still-mistrusted science of psychology; and he was a pioneer in juror profiling. Witnesses, too, received meticulous scrutiny, as he became the first lawyer to use private investigators on background checks. Preparation of this caliber meant that he had never had to go fishing for answers on cross-examination; he already knew what was coming. So complete was his mastery of witnesses, that noted legal scholar, Francis Wellman, declared, "Earl Rogers invented the art of cross-examination as it is now practiced."[8] (Years later, Erle Stanley Gardner reputedly modeled his fictional attorney Perry Mason on Rogers.)

Rogers' career soared like a comet, then slowly fizzled into painful oblivion. Like White, he was a hostage to the bottle. Alcoholism ruined him. He would stagger from the sanitarium to the courtroom, win another astounding verdict, and then lurch back to the hospital bed. The victories all added to the myth of invincibility that surrounded his name. But the battle with the booze was one fight that not even Earl Rogers could win. He died, penniless and alone, in a cheap Los Angeles rooming house on February 22, 1922. He was just 52 years old.

5

Duty Calls

It all begins with a letter in the mail. You open the envelope, study the contents, and see the heading: JURY SUMMONS. Congratulations! You are one of the almost 32 million Americans who, in 2006, received this call to civic duty. As a direct result of those letters, an estimated 148,558 juries were impaneled in state courts (federal courts upped the annual total by another 5,463 trials.)[1] Depending on one's point of view, this summons is either an inconvenience of the greatest possible magnitude or it's an opportunity to glimpse the inner workings of the American legal system and to perform one's civic duty.

On the appointed day those summoned for jury duty attend the courthouse and there—along with dozens of other citizens—become a member of the jury pool. The only characteristics all the attendees share is that they are over 18 years of age, on some kind of electoral register or have a driver's license, and are not a convicted felon. Apart from that, each prospective juror's name has been plucked purely by random. And that's the idea; to obtain as wide a cross section of the general public as possible.

Being a member of the potential juror pool by no means guarantees actually participating in a trial. Courts routinely summons many more potential jurors than they need. This is to cover for no-shows (expect another, much sterner letter in the mail) and those individuals whose occupations generally exempt them from jury service. Traditionally this group includes community-based occupations such as doctors, firefighters, and anyone associated with the criminal justice system (including the police). These are the people who keep the country running on a day-to-day basis. Other exemptions may be granted on grounds of medical or financial hardship.

Those whose names are then selected from the pool proceed to a courtroom where the judge, or possibly the attorneys for both sides, will assess each person's fitness to sit on that particular jury. This process is called *voir dire*.

Once all parties are satisfied, 12 jurors are then impaneled and the trial can begin. It is each juror's duty to listen to the facts of the case and to deliver a verdict on these facts alone. But it is important to remember that there are 12 distinct personalities in the jury room, and the truth is that no one, not even the savviest legal professional, can predict every jury outcome. Sometimes there is just no accounting for human nature.

In 1981 a New York electrical engineer named Bernhard Goetz was attacked in the Canal Street subway station by three youths who attempted to steal his jacket. When Goetz resisted, he was beaten to the ground and badly injured his knee. Of the three attackers only one was arrested. Much to Goetz's disgust, the prisoner got off lightly; charged with just criminal mischief for ripping his jacket. Following this incident Goetz applied for a permit to carry a handgun, on the basis that he frequently carried expensive equipment and large sums of cash on his person. His application was denied. Infuriated by this rejection, Goetz bought a gun and began carrying it illegally.

Three years later, on December 22, 1984, while riding the subway, the 36-year-old Goetz was approached by four black youths, one of who demanded $5. Goetz's response was to yank a .38 Smith & Wesson revolver from a special quick-draw holster and begin spraying bullets. As two of the youths fled, Goetz shot them in the back. One, Darrell Cabey, 19, fell. Goetz approached him and said, "You seem to be all right; here's another,"[2] firing a second open-nosed bullet that severed Cabey's spinal cord. Then Goetz calmly alighted from the subway car and disappeared.

Nine days later—after a torrent of newspaper coverage—the man dubbed the "Subway Vigilante"[3] surrendered himself to the authorities

In jury trials 12 jurors are selected from a pool through a process called *voir dire*, in which attorneys for plaintiff and defendant question potential jurors about their background and beliefs.
AP Photo/Brett Coomer, Pool

in Concord, New Hampshire. Goetz was later extradited to New York. Following several lengthy confessions he was charged with 13 various offenses, ranging from attempted murder to criminal possession of a gun.

Bringing the case to court took more than two years. Selecting a jury for such an obviously volatile trial proved almost as laborious, as neither side wanted to concede any advantage in this most critical phase of the judicial process. The jury selection process began on March 23, 1987. When Judge Stephen G. Crane asked the potential jurors if they had ever heard of Bernhard Goetz, defense lawyer Barry Slotnick observed dryly, "People who don't know about this case have been in [*sic*] Mars for the past three years."[4] Slotnick's sarcasm only highlighted

(continues on page 67)

VOIR DIRE

Voir dire—from the Old French for "to speak the truth"—is one of the most important phases of any trial. It is the selection process whereby potential jurors are questioned by attorneys from both sides about their background, experiences, and, most critically, their beliefs. From the answers given, both sides form an opinion as to whether that person can weigh the evidence fairly and objectively. The idea is to ferret out prejudice and bias in the search to obtain a fair and impartial jury. But this tells only part of the story. In reality, both sides—prosecution and defense—are hoping to stack the jury in their favor. This is why, in the opinion of many attorneys, jury selection is the single most important procedure in the entire trial process. It becomes a battle of wits, with both sides constantly maneuvering to gain some perceived advantage. Often the *voir dire* process, with its serpentine twists and turns, can be as dramatic as the trial itself.

Traditionally, American attorneys have had much latitude in conducting *voir dire*. As the questioning proceeds, an attorney can challenge a prospective juror "for cause" if that person expresses a bias against that attorney's case. For instance, say the suit is tobacco-related, and a prospective juror states her belief that her late husband's lung cancer resulted from the cigarettes he smoked; it is overwhelmingly likely that this person would be challenged "for cause." If the judge agreed—and it's hard to imagine that one wouldn't—then that person would be excused. Each side also has a limited number of "peremptory" challenges for which no reasons are required. These are used sparingly and are usually inspired by gut instinct, a sense, rather than anything expressed, that the person would not be favorably disposed toward that side's argument.

In cases where the defendant, if convicted, might be subject to capital punishment, a special rider is added to the *voir dire* process; the jurors need to be "death qualified." This requires that they have no moral objection to the imposition of the death penalty. Anyone stating otherwise would be automatically excluded from the panel.

As the stakes rise, so does the intensity of *voir dire*. In big civil suits, most attorneys employ jury consultants. These are specialist companies that call on huge databases and demographic research, all designed to provide an insight into human predictability. Depending on the financial resources (and the ethics) of the hiring attorney, these companies will provide a detailed report of every aspect of a prospective juror's life. This might include income, domestic status, indebtedness, political leanings, hobbies, even where that person buys his or her clothes. From these scraps of information, the jury consultants piece together a psychological profile that will—or so they claim—predict how that particular person is likely to vote. Generalizations abound. The wealthy are thought to be pro-prosecution, while those further down the economic ladder are more sympathetic to the defense. Gender plays a part as well, with some studies suggesting that women are more disposed to the defense, while men lean more toward the prosecution.

In some instances, jury consultants will arrange for a "shadow" jury to be impaneled, one that reflects similarities to the real jury. It is the job of this jury to follow the trial and to give the lawyers feedback on the various developments. From this, appropriate strategies can be mapped out. Once all this information has been digested, the attorney may decide to exercise a peremptory challenge.

When it comes to *voir dire*, everyone is looking for an edge, and there have been numerous examples of misuse and even abuse. This can be especially troublesome in cases where the financial resources of one side vastly outweigh those of the opposition. Eventually, from a juror panel that might have initially numbered in the hundreds, the whittling down process continues until there are 12 jurors acceptable to both sides. These will then be impaneled and sworn in as the jury.

Bernhard Goetz arrives at Central Booking in Manhattan wearing handcuffs and escorted by police in March 1985. *AP Photo*

(continued from page 63)

the problems involved with sitting a jury. Trying to weed out precon-
ceptions is difficult, especially in such a high-profile case as the Subway
Shootings. There were millions of New Yorkers who regarded Goetz as
a hero. Probably just as many thought he was a gun-happy psychopath.
This wasn't going to be easy.

Barry Slotnick, though, was used to tough cases, and he was used to
unpopular clients. While still in his 20s he had represented the reputed
New York crime boss Joseph A. Colombo, and was actually standing
only a yard away from Colombo on June 28, 1971, when the latter was
gunned down at a rally in Columbus Circle. Slotnick wasn't fazed by
the experience. He continued to argue appeals before the United States
Supreme Court on behalf of the comatose Colombo, right up until the
latter's death in 1978. Ordinarily Slotnick charged $350 per hour for
his services. Here, he defended Goetz **pro bono**, believing that the case
raised a fundamental social issue: Does the citizen have the right to
defend himself or does the law mandate submission?

It took 10 days of hard questioning before the eight-man, four-
woman jury was impaneled. Most observers concentrated more on the
jury's racial makeup—10 white and two black—and speculated what
impact this might have on the outcome. Slotnick probably preferred
to concentrate on the fact that six of the jurors had themselves been
the victims of crime, three of them subway related. Viewed from a
distance it appeared as if the defense had edged the crucial *voir dire*
phase of the trial.

After a further delay for various motions, on April 27, 1987, it was
time for Assistant District Attorney Gregory Waples to make the opening presentation. He outlined the salient facts, then told the jury members that Goetz was "not a typical New Yorker, not a reasonable person
such as yourself," but rather someone with "a twisted and self-righteous
sense of right and wrong . . . an emotional powder keg, one spark away
from explosion."[5] To drive home this point, Waples highlighted Goetz's
refusal to wear gloves, even on the coldest winter day, so that he might
remain "fast on the draw"[6] should trouble arise. Such an obsession, the
prosecutor reasoned, was far more likely to lead Goetz into conflict

rather than avoid it. According to Waples, the victims had been merely panhandling when Goetz exploded for no reason and opened fire.

The defense saw things in an entirely different light. Slotnick's opening statement portrayed Bernhard Goetz as "Mr. Everyman," just an ordinary guy who twice before had suffered at the hands of muggers, a victim so traumatized that when four "vicious predators"[7] approached him, he pulled out a .38 caliber revolver and shot them. Slotnick cranked up the rhetoric. "The four muggers got exactly what the law allows," he said. "They went about their life stealing, cheating and robbing other people. When you go and rob someone, you assume the risk someone may fight back."[8]

Slotnick next launched a vitriolic assault on the character and credibility of James Ramseur, one of the alleged assailants. Five months after the Goetz incident, Ramseur had been arrested for participating in the savage gang-rape of a pregnant woman. So heavy-handed and graphic did Slotnick's depiction of this rape become that it drew a sharp rebuke from Justice Stephen Crane, "Why don't you get off this, Mr. Slotnick."[9]

But the damage had been done. The impression of the four black youths as rampaging sadists was firmly implanted in the jury's mind. This skillful defense manipulation of proceedings went a stage further when one of the People's witnesses, Detective Michael Clark, referred to "the four victims on the train." Slotnick was on his feet immediately. "Your Honor, I would object to the characterization of the 'victim.' That's a decision the jury will have to make."[10] Surprisingly, the prosecution yielded the point, agreeing to the much meeker term "young men."[11] It was another small but important victory for the defense: Slowly Bernhard Goetz was being turned into the victim of this attack, not the perpetrator.

At the core of the prosecution's case was a taped confession that Goetz had made while in custody. Because Goetz exercised his constitutional right to silence and did not take the stand, this was the jury's only opportunity to hear him speak. In a rambling, two-hour account Goetz gave his version of the attack. It contained many damaging statements. Most incriminating of all was his clearly expressed intention "to murder them, to hurt them, to make them suffer as much as possible."[12] He'd been driven to this response, he said, because of resentment over the way they were playing him, "Like a cat plays with a mouse."[13]

Several witnesses from the subway train testified. Through careful questioning Slotnick succeeded in drawing admissions from some that the action had happened so quickly as to impair their recollection of what actually occurred. In particular, Slotnick created doubt about the actual number of shots fired. The intention here was to undermine the prosecution's claim that Goetz had cold-bloodedly stood over Cabey and fired the fifth and most damaging shot. Through shrewd questioning, Slotnick managed to achieve at least part of his desired aim. Some of the witnesses recalled that all the shots had been fired in quick succession, and that Cabey's spinal injury had resulted from random gunfire, not a willful shot.

Leaving his partner, Mark Baker, to deal with the legal technicalities, Slotnick dictated courtroom strategy. In an attempt to divert the jury's attention from his client's undeniably odd character and instead to focus it on the alleged assailants, Slotnick attacked each gang member in turn. James Ramseur was portrayed as a monster who had, said Slotnick, "left [his pregnant victim] . . . bleeding on the rooftop landing." Ramseur's cockiness under cross-examination made Slotnick's task that much easier.

Another of the alleged assailants, Troy Canty, provided much stiffer resistance. Slotnick warned the jury against being fooled by Canty, who came into court nattily attired in a suit and tie. Instead, he hammered on about "four menacing foes,"[14] holding up, for the jury, poster-sized enlargements of photos of each in their street clothes.

There were times when Slotnick's strategy toyed with the bounds of acceptability. One contentious interlude hinged upon his hiring of Joseph Quirk, a ballistics expert, to re-create the crime scene in court. For the purposes of this demonstration, Slotnick had engaged the services of four black youths, dressed like street toughs, to act out the parts of the attackers. Had the defense only been interested in demonstrating bullet paths then the color of the assistants would have been immaterial, but the sight of four black teenagers jostling Quirk, a white man, was highly inflammatory. So much so, that Judge Crane ordered Slotnick to use court employees in future, should he need to carry out any further demonstrations.

Slowly and inexorably, Slotnick recast Bernhard Goetz as victim, not vigilante. It was an impressive feat of reconstruction. Judge Crane, in his final charge to the jury, first clarified the law on justified violence in defense of one's person. Significantly, though, he urged the jury to engage in a frank and open discussion among themselves. "When you are in the jury room, listen to each other," said Judge Crane. "Without violating your judgment or conscience, your verdict in this case must be unanimous."[15] The jury got the case at 1:20 P.M. on June 12. When, at the end of the day, it was clear that no verdict had been reached, the jury members were driven to a hotel where they were sequestered for the night.

This was a process repeated over the next three days as the jury wrestled with the evidence. Finally, at 4:10 P.M. on June 16, after more than 30 hours of deliberation, the jury was ready. James M. Hurley, the jury foreman, stood to deliver a verdict that would resonate around the world. Twelve times he intoned "Not guilty." Only once did he respond "Guilty"—to a charge of criminal possession of a weapon in the third degree.

After the verdicts were handed down, several of the jurors reportedly asked if Goetz could sign their jury service certificates, but by this time he had left the courthouse. Shortly afterward the jurors, many flashing victory signs with their fingers, left the court by bus. Their civic duty was over. Their media duty was now about to begin.

The comments they made provide an illuminating insight into the jury process. For instance, many jurors expressed their belief that neither side had made an overwhelming case. It was clear, though, that from the outset of their deliberations there was near-universal empathy for the defendant. One of the jurors, Diana Serpe, told how they had conducted 35 separate votes over the four days, and in not one of them did anybody "ever cast a guilty vote on the major charges."[16] Another juror, James Moseley, stressed that the entire panel had virtually discounted Goetz's taped confession. Instead, they placed far greater weight on the words of Andrea Reid, a black passenger in Goetz's subway car, who had testified, "Those four got what they deserved."[17]

JURY TAMPERING

Jury tampering is the crime of attempting to influence a jury through other means than the evidence presented in court. This may take the form of conversations about the case outside the court, offering bribes, making threats, or asking acquaintances to interfere with a juror. A juror includes any person who is a member of any jury, including a grand jury, impaneled by any court or by any public servant authorized by law to impanel a jury. The term *juror* also includes any person who has been summoned or whose name has been drawn to attend as a prospective juror. Lawyers are expected to abide by a code of ethics that forbids them to talk to a juror outside the courtroom. This code even covers chance meetings in, for example, an elevator.

In the past, most attempts at jury-tampering involved some kind of personal contact. But the digital age has changed all that. In 2007 when Chandra Bozelko, 35, of Orange, Connecticut, found herself on trial for credit card fraud, larceny, and identify theft, several members of the jury suddenly began receiving phone calls from an anonymous caller, who wished to talk about the innocence of Bozelko. It turned out that the caller was Bozelko herself. She had logged onto a spoofing Web site that would conceal her phone number on caller ID and disguise her voice in real time, using electronic means. The jurors were unimpressed. They convicted Bozelko anyway, and she was sentenced to 10 years. When prosecutors heard of the calls, they hunted around, found a computer at her parents' residence that led them straight to the spoofing site, and slapped her with additional counts of harassment and tampering with evidence. Ms. Bozelko, who had earlier gained national notoriety in the running world after it was discovered that she had only run the last mile in each of six marathons in which she allegedly competed, is currently fighting these latest charges from behind bars at York Correctional Institute.

With so much interest in the trial and such a controversial outcome, everyone wanted to interview the jurors. Speaking that same night on the ABC-News television program *Nightline*, Michael Axelrod told how he and his fellow jurors simply concentrated on the facts and the situation, adding that to suggest "that this is a racial thing is just a bunch of garbage."[18]

Had Goetz been convicted on all charges, he would have been facing a 30-year jail term. As it was, on October 19, he was sentenced to six months in jail, plus a $5,000 fine, and four and one-half years' probation. A subsequent review increased the jail sentence to one year. He served eight months. In 1996, in a civil trial, Cabey was awarded $43 million damages against Goetz.

When the jurors in the Goetz trial received their summonses in the mail, none could have realized what the next few months held in store. The pressures bearing down on them were enormous, as they attempted to unravel the evidence in one of the most controversial cases in recent decades. Many were dissatisfied with the outcome; others felt vindicated. It was a trial that produced no winners, and perhaps the final word is best left with one of the jurors, Catherine Brody: "We weren't proud of the verdict, but proud of the fact that we did our job well."[19]

6

The Color
of Money

There is an old saying in legal circles: "You can't convict a million dollars." And there is plenty of evidence to suggest that the deep-pocketed defendant does get a different kind of justice compared to that dispensed to those who aren't wealthy. When, in 1917, Blanca de Saulles resolved an irksome child custody battle with her ex-husband, John, by driving to his Long Island house and pumping five bullets into him, her passage through the American judicial system was certainly smoothed by the fact that she came from a wealthy Chilean family that had produced no fewer than six presidents of that country. Blanca's pricey legal team was able to convince the jury that their client had been insane at the time of the killing and she walked free. This was far from being an isolated case. Since the beginning of the 20th century, plenty of other well-heeled murder charge defendants such as Harry Thaw, Candace Mossler, Cullen Davis, O.J. Simpson, and more recently the New York millionaire Robert Durst, have won the kinds of acquittals that overworked public defenders can only dream about.

Whatever outrage these verdicts might provoke in some quarters, it needs to be balanced against one important consideration: In the vast majority of cases the scales of justice are weighted heavily in favor of the prosecution. In terms of resources and manpower, the state holds all the aces. They have tens, possibly hundreds, of investigative personnel at their disposal; they can call on the finest forensic laboratories; summon as many expert witnesses as necessary; and all on the taxpayer's dime. If the defendant wants that extra chromatographic analysis, then it means digging into his or her own pocket. Forensic science doesn't come cheap.

Some argue that money merely evens up the playing field. And there can be no doubt that when a well-financed defense team swings into action, it does put extra pressure on the prosecution to perform. Whenever they come up short, somebody is sure to spout that old "million dollar" cliché. But all rules are made to be broken. And every now and then the state manages to confound the cynics and demonstrate that even the heftiest bank balance is no guarantee of dodging justice.

On the evening of October 11, 1963, a woman named Naomi Markowitz went to a Brooklyn police station to file a missing person's report. Her husband, Rubin—everyone called him Ruby—had disappeared the previous afternoon. This wasn't like Ruby at all, she explained; normally her husband was regular as clockwork. And there was something else. Earlier that day, a friend of Ruby's told her that he had spotted the missing man's car parked on First Avenue near 64th Street. As police officers took the details, something didn't sound right. Naomi was hesitant at first, describing her 40-year-old husband as a $90 a week grocery clerk, but gradually it emerged that Ruby Markowitz had a second source of income; he ran a bookmaking business and, furthermore, just recently he'd pocketed a small fortune on the 1963 World Series.

When the Dodgers, led by Sandy Koufax, swept the Yankees in four games, baseball watchers rubbed their eyes in disbelief. So did Mark Fein. The 32-year-old president of Fein Industries, a thriving company that manufactured tin cans and cardboard boxes, might have been able to run a successful business, but he was a lousy gambler. All through the World Series, Fein had plunged money on the Yankees. Each defeat only pushed him further into the hole. By the end of game four, he owed thousands of dollars to various bookmakers. One of them was Ruby Markowitz.

As the son of a multimillionaire, Fein could afford the high life. With his glamorous heiress wife, Nancy, and their three children, he lived in a $65,000 cooperative duplex apartment at 1095 Park Avenue. The family had a housekeeper and a nurse to tend to their every need.

Fein drove a gleaming white Lincoln Continental. It might have been his father, Irving, who controlled the corporate purse strings, but he'd made it clear that, eventually, full control of the company would fall into Mark's grasp. Until that happy day, Mark was content to live the life of a free-spending playboy. Most of his money went on gambling. Before switching his bets to Ruby, Mark had racked up debts of $60,000 with other bookies. He'd managed to pay off those commitments, but word on the grapevine was that Fein and two of his betting buddies owed Ruby close to $24,000 after a string of catastrophic wagers. The police knew this because they'd found a list of Ruby's customers and Fein's name figured prominently.

The first that Fein knew of this police interest was when they came to visit him on October 14. Initially Fein appeared bemused when they mentioned Rubin Markowitz but then a detective showed him a picture of the missing man. "Oh, you must mean *Ruby* Markowitz,"[1] said Fein. He admitted knowing Ruby but only as a source for hard-to-find sports tickets. He denied having any gambling dealings with Markowitz or seeing him on October 10, the day of his disappearance.

After a few days Fein underwent a change of heart. Accompanied by a lawyer, he went to the police and admitted that he had wagered with Ruby, and had seen him on the afternoon of October 10, between 3:30 and 4:00 P.M., to settle a gambling debt. The two had met in Ruby's car, which was parked outside a gas station at First Avenue and 61st Street. There was another man in the car, said Fein, "About 45 years old, a white man with a dark complexion, wearing a gray suit and a fedora. He needed a shave and looked, uh, possibly Italian."[2] Fein had not said anything to the Mafia-like stranger, just paid his gambling debt and walked off. That was the last time he'd seen Ruby Markowitz.

And nobody did see any more of Ruby Markowitz until just after dawn on November 8, 1963, when his body was dragged from the Harlem River. His wrists and ankles were bound with rope, and he had been shot four times in the head and chest. Robbery obviously wasn't the motive, because the police found $441 in his pockets, plus an address book.

In the weeks since Fein's interview, detectives had expended a great deal of time and effort searching for the "possibly Italian" man that Fein had described. Friends of the dead man dismissed any notion of Ruby consorting with Mafia mobsters or loan sharks; it was not his style at all. Frustrated detectives agreed. This left them with just one line of investigation: the fact that the last person to see Ruby Markowitz alive was Mark Fein.

For this reason, they kept hammering away at the wealthy business-man. One day after Markowitz was fished out of the river, the *New York Daily News* ran a story headlined, "Clerk Jekyll & Bookie Hyde Found Slain in 24g Puzzler." Further on in the piece, Mark Fein's name cropped up, as did the tantalizing tidbit that he had paid off Markowitz the $24,000 on the day of his disappearance. Information of this caliber could only have come from a police leak. When detectives dug into Ruby's phone records, they noticed that a large numbers of calls had been placed from an apartment at 406 East 63rd Street, close to where Fein said he'd met Ruby. It transpired that the $178 a month apartment was rented to a William Weissman, whose rental application stated that he worked for Fein Industries. Except that personnel records at Fein Industries showed no Weissman on the payroll.

When detectives phoned Fein at his Park Avenue home, to clarify this matter, they were given the cold shoulder. On lawyer's advice, Fein was refusing to speak to them. His supercilious manner toward the police, or indeed anyone whom he considered his social inferior, rankled with the detectives. When they tried to make enquiries at Fein Industries, Fein protested to high officials that he was being harassed and he wanted it to stop. But things were just about to get a lot worse for the Park Avenue millionaire.

Another phone number on Ruby's records was traced to an apart-ment on 73rd Street, and a 37-year-old woman who called herself Gloria Kendal. Over the course of a colorful career littered with arrests for prostitution, Carmela Lazarus had assumed a score of different aliases, but Gloria Kendal is the name with which she achieved lasting notoriety. When she wasn't working as a prostitute, Gloria doubled as a madam, arranging for women to visit wealthy men and then taking a cut of the proceeds. When interviewed, she denied knowing anybody called Mark Fein. But detectives reckoned she was lying. Although they strongly suspected that Fein was somehow connected to Markowitz's death, they couldn't picture the bespectacled, puny businessman carrying out the hit himself. Far more likely, they thought, was that Fein had hired someone to get rid of the troublesome bookie. And that would require underworld contacts, perhaps someone like Gloria Kendal.

Gloria was saying nothing. Her intransigence was countered by a novel police strategy. They began putting the squeeze on her line of work. Clients were busted and their women friends suddenly found themselves the subject of intense police surveillance. Over the next couple of months, as the money dried up and the bills began to mount, Gloria's hazy memory suddenly cleared. But not in the way that investigators expected.

On February 20, 1964, she met with homicide detective Frank Lyons and dropped a bombshell. "Mark Fein murdered Ruby. He shot him. I saw the body in a trunk."[3] Gloria didn't spare any detail, exploding Fein's façade of a home-loving family man and exposing every fact of Fein's life to the merciless glare of the media.

That evening, Fein and his wife had just exited their apartment block, en route to a restaurant, when detectives marched up and placed him under arrest. He was hauled off, hollering at the top of his lungs that he was being kidnapped. Facing a charge of first-degree murder and a possible date with the electric chair, Fein did the smart thing and hired William Kleinman, one of New York's finest criminal lawyers.

With the Fein family fortune at work—Irving Fein would later issue a $25,000 reward for information leading to the conviction of the "true murderer"[4] of Markowitz—skepticism was high over chances of a guilty verdict. Even Detective Lyons had his doubts. "Everybody told me Fein was sure to get away,"[5] he said, speaking later. Lyons' qualms worsened considerably on July 1, when Fein was unexpectedly freed on $50,000 bail. It was the first time since 1929 that a first-degree murder defendant had been bailed in New York County.

The prosecution knew they were in for the fight of their life. Virtually their entire case hinged on the testimony of an admitted prostitute. There would be no prizes for guessing what strategy the defense would adopt: an all-out attack on the credibility of Gloria Kendal. Responsibility for the prosecution rested in the hands of Assistant District Attorney Vincent J. Dermody. He had a long track record of success in difficult cases. In 1941 he had been hired right out of law school by former New York governor Thomas Dewey, to join his legendary Gangbusters, a team of government attorneys dedicated to breaking organized crime in New York City. But for the last 15 years Dermody had been the prosecutor in scores of homicide trials. Murder was his specialty. And he wasn't about to let Fein off the hook.

The trial began in a Manhattan courtroom in October 1964. Dermody opened by outlining Fein's betting activities. After a succession of witnesses had paraded through, linking Fein to the deceased bookie, it was time for Dermody to produce his ace-in-the-hole. Gloria Kendal, an attractive redhead, drew plenty of admiring glances from the all-male jury as she walked to the stand in a stylishly cut outfit. Dermody made no attempt to camouflage Gloria's dubious antecedents; better it come from the prosecution than the defense, was his reasoning. He had Gloria explain how she'd met Fein in 1960 through a stockbroker client of hers, and how, since that time, she had seen Fein every week or so. Fein paid her $400–$600 per month for her services. Sometimes he would take male friends to her apartment and Gloria would arrange other girls for the occasion, with Fein picking up the tab.

In May 1963 Fein "asked me if I could loan him any money," Gloria said, because "he had lost a lot of money, I believe on baseball."[6] She had offered him a few hundred dollars, but he said that would not help because he owed $60,000. She and some friends gave him $4,600, which he'd repaid in September 1963. It was around this time that she started meeting Fein at the 63rd Street apartment, and it was from there that he telephoned her on October 10, 1963. He sounded flustered and asked if she could come over immediately. When Gloria replied that she was busy and tried to put him off, Fein became more urgent, saying, "I can't wait, Gloria. I have to see you right away!"[7] Wearily, Gloria agreed.

When she walked into the apartment she saw a large trunk in the middle of the living room. "'What do you think is in the trunk?'" she quoted Fein as asking. She said she did not know, and he told her: "It's the body of a dead man, my bookmaker, Ruby."[8] Gloria told how Fein went on to explain that he'd owed the dead man close to $24,000. "I met him at 4 o'clock," Fein had said. "He came up here. We were talking. We had words and I shot him."[9] When Gloria queried whether Markowitz was

Special prosecutor Thomas E. Dewey holds up his right hand as he is sworn in by Supreme Court Justice Philip J. McCook in New York City in 1935. Dewey's Gangbusters were dedicated to fighting organized crime in New York City. One member of the crime-fighting team of attorneys, Vincent J. Dermody, went on to serve as prosecutor in the Mark Fein murder trial in 1964. *AP Photo*

definitely dead, Fein raised the lid of the trunk, "exposing part of an arm, some new clothesline and some white material that looked like a shirt."[10] Fein had then looked imploringly at her. "Please, Gloria, help me."[11]

And help him she did. First, she called two friends, David Broudy and Geri Boxer, and asked them to come over. They agreed. Fein used the hiatus to rent a station wagon over the phone, which he went to pick up in person. When Broudy and Boxer arrived, they helped heft the heavy trunk—Markowitz weighed around 200 pounds—downstairs to where the station wagon was waiting. Leaving Fein on the sidewalk, Gloria and her two friends cruised around in the station wagon for about half an hour until they stopped at a quiet spot on the bank of the

Harlem River. There, the trio carried the trunk to the edge and pushed it over into the water. Hungry from their efforts, the trio went to a French restaurant on West 49th Street. Broudy, a cabbie, later returned the station wagon to the rental agency.

DEWEY'S GANGBUSTERS

In 1935 a New York grand jury was summoned to investigate the city's racketeering problem. It uncovered evidence of an organized crime ring, operating on a hitherto unimagined scale, with tentacles that stretched nationwide. The grand jury demanded the appointment of a special prosecutor whose sole mission would be to pursue these gangsters and bring them to justice. At the fourth time of asking—tackling the most homicidal mobsters in America was not everyone's cup of tea—Governor Harold H. Lehman finally found someone willing to tackle the dangerous job.

Thomas E. Dewey had risen to prominence as the chief assistant U.S. attorney for the Southern District of New York. At the time of his appointment, he was 33 years old, ambitious, and single-minded. His brief was to bring down what New York newspapers luridly dubbed Murder, Inc., the enforcing wing of a ruthless crime syndicate headed up by Charles "Lucky" Luciano. This national crime syndicate, established in the days of prohibition, ran loan-sharking, gambling, narcotics, and just about every other illegal money-making enterprise. To fight them, Dewey assembled a 60-strong team of like-minded prosecutors, assistants, and investigators that became known as the Gangbusters.

The mob quickly came to fear and respect Dewey. When one hoodlum, "Dutch" Schultz, who had been hounded out of New York by Dewey, angrily declared his intention to assassinate the popular special prosecutor, the board of Murder Inc. stepped in to avert what would have been a public relations disaster. That night, October 23, 1935, Schultz was gunned down by two Murder, Inc., hit men in the men's room of a New Jersey restaurant.

As expected, Kleinman tore into Gloria like an enraged pit bull. He accused her of lying, of switching stories—true—of doing deals with the prosecutor to avoid charges herself—true again—but mostly

(continues on page 84)

Over the next two years, with Dewey at the helm, the Gangbusters gained national fame, securing 72 convictions against just one acquittal. The biggest prize of all came in 1936 when Luciano, who was personally prosecuted by Dewey, found himself in court on charges of forcing women into prostitution. Dewey demolished Luciano on the stand, exposing him repeatedly as a brazen liar, as he tried to explain how he managed to acquire such fabulous wealth. When it came time to address the jury, Dewey described Luciano's testimony as "a shocking, disgusting display of sanctimonious perjury—at the end of which I am sure not one of you had a doubt that before you stood not a gambler, not a bookmaker, but the greatest gangster in America."[12] The jury agreed and Luciano was convicted on all counts and sentenced to between 30 and 50 years' imprisonment. In 1941 Dewey's team broke the back of Murder, Inc., with a large trial that saw seven of the organization's top killers sent to the electric chair.

Like many lawyers before him, Dewey used the courtroom as a stepping-stone into the political arena. Few did it with greater success. Dewey parlayed his courtroom success into a political career that propelled him to three terms as governor of New York state (1943–1955), and two unsuccessful tilts at the White House, as Republican candidate in 1944 and 1948. When Dewey's third term as governor expired in 1955, he retired from public life and his days in the limelight were over. In the 1960s he reportedly declined a seat on the Supreme Court, preferring to devote his efforts to his lucrative private practice. On March 16, 1971, the man who was arguably the most successful prosecutor of the 20th century died at age 68 while vacationing in Miami, Florida.

THE COURT-MARTIAL

The American court-martial is a military court, held in accordance with the Uniform Code of Military Justice, to try members of the armed services for crimes alleged to have been committed either in peacetime or in war. A panel of officers sits in judgment, while both the prosecuting and defending counsel are military lawyers, although the accused may elect, at his own expense, to be represented by a civilian lawyer. Many of the offenses covered by a court-martial closely resemble civilian crimes such as theft, drug dealing, and fraud. Others, like cowardice, desertion, and insubordination, are purely military offenses. The gravest of these is war crimes.

On the morning of March 16, 1968, a unit of the United States 11th Light Infantry Brigade moved unopposed into the Vietnamese hamlet of My Lai. By midday almost 500 inhabitants had been massacred. All the victims were unarmed civilians: women, babies, elderly men. By chance, the scenes of blood-drenched carnage were recorded by an Army cameraman, and it was his pictures that revealed the horror of My Lai to the world.

An Army inquiry into the incident resulted in charges of murder against several participants, but evidence suggested that the majority of blame for the tragedy could be laid at the door of a single platoon commander—Lieutenant William Calley.

In November 1970 Calley faced a court-martial, charged with ordering the murder of 109 Vietnamese citizens. Calley's defense was that standby of soldiers since time immemorial, "I was only acting on orders."

After a four-month court-martial, and almost 80 deliberations, the six-officer jury—five of whom had served in Vietnam—found Calley guilty of the premeditated murder of 22 villagers at My Lai. Calley avoided the death penalty, but was sentenced to life imprisonment. On August 20, 1971, the sentence was reduced to 20 years. Just three years later, Calley was paroled. The officer who gave Calley his orders, Captain Ernest Medina, was acquitted of any complicity in the slaughter.

Former Army Lieutenant William Calley, clad in civilian dress, leaves the Fort Benning military stockade to appear before a judge to appeal his 1970 conviction for the murder of 22 villagers in My Lai, Vietnam. The appeal was denied, but Calley was paroled in 1974. *AP Photo/Joe Holloway Jr.*

(continued from page 81)

he attempted to turn his cross-examination into the trial of Gloria Kendal, portraying her as a "diabolically clever creature"[13] whose evidence wasn't worth a candle. And in this endeavor he failed notably. For despite all the insults, Gloria stood firm and acquitted herself well on the stand.

She found a strong ally in David Broudy. His testimony supported Gloria's in every respect. He told of returning several times to the apartment to help Gloria clean and redecorate. During the course of these visits, Fein told him that the man in the trunk was an intruder whom he had shot. Broudy said he had no reason to doubt Fein. Geri Boxer, too, was clear in her testimony. She said the sequence of events had unfolded just as Gloria stated.

The corroboration for Gloria's story kept coming. Donald Galka, the rental agent for the apartment block, testified that, on the afternoon in question, he had seen Gloria and Fein in the lobby of the apartment block, struggling with the trunk. He was positive in his identifications.

All the defense could offer was a weak attempt at an alibi. Nancy Fein took the stand, to swear that, on October 10, 1963, her husband arrived home "between 6 and 6:30,"[14] at which time, the prosecution alleged, Fein was at a garage, picking up a station wagon he had rented earlier by phone. This contradicted the claim of Kendal, Boxer, and Broudy, that Fein was in the apartment with them at 6:00 P.M. Fein, exercising his constitutional right to silence, declined to take the stand.

In summation, William Kleinman, said it was inconceivable that "a mere $7,000"[15] (Fein's share of the $23,890 owed to Markowitz) could be a motive for murder. Fein was not only wealthy in his own right, but married to a wife with a considerable fortune; he had no reason to kill for such a trifling sum. But mostly, Kleinman begged the jury not to condemn his client on the word of a lowlife like Gloria Kendal.

In response, Dermody told the jury that he couldn't pick the witnesses; it was his duty to present them in court. Gloria, he freely admitted, had "the morals of an alley cat,"[16] but did that make her evidence any less believable? He asked the jury to "analyze her testimony,"[17] and to reach their own conclusions. As for that preposterous defense claim that someone as rich as Fein would not deign to kill for such a paltry sum, Dermody just scoffed. Everyone, he told the jury—even a millionaire—has their breaking point. Fein had amassed total gambling debts of $60,000. And the bookies were calling in their markers. That was motive enough.

On November 25, 1964, after 20 hours of deliberation, the jury finally came back with a verdict: guilty of second-degree murder. Mark Fein seemed stunned. All the blood drained from his face, taking with it the air of smug arrogance that had endured for every previous day of the trial. Only now did it register that his family's wealth had failed him and that he was going to prison for a long time. Kleinman had done his best and kept Fein out of the electric chair; now it was up to the court. Several months later, after a hearing to establish whether a retrial was necessary had overturned defense claims that there had been no body in the trunk, just heavy weights put there by Kendal and her cohorts in order to blackmail the unsuspecting millionaire, Fein was sentenced to 30 years to life.

Convictions in cases such as these are hard to win, and harder still to maintain through the appeal process. Despite throwing tens of thousands of dollars at the judicial system, Fein ran out of options and he had to do the time. His last desperate gamble had failed. Paying off Ruby Markowitz would have been so much less expensive for all concerned.

The
Media Circus

In the media world, murders are good copy. Sometimes, they make really great copy. Usually this occurs when either the victim or the defendant is someone socially prominent or wealthy. Then circulation figures can soar into the stratosphere. From Harry Thaw at the beginning of the 20th century, to Bruno Hauptmann in the 1930s, right through to the travails of O.J. Simpson, newspaper editors and, more recently, TV newsroom directors have tapped into this public fascination with the rich and famous. Over the years, as the coverage has become more extensive and intrusive, complaints have multiplied over how some of these stories reach the public ear. Journalists under attack for perceived excesses have usually sought refuge in the First Amendment, which enshrines the right to free speech. But what of the defendant? He or she has rights too, and fundamental among these is the right to a fair trial. The distinctions are hazy at best. At times they have been trampled into oblivion. For most of the first half of the 20th century it was the press that held sway when it came to reporting trials. Radio had some impact, but power resided mainly with the newspaper editor. This was especially true on a local level. Hostile coverage not only prejudiced popular opinion against the defendant, but it did it in the very area from which a jury was to be selected.

Then came television. Between 1950 and 1960 the number of TV sets in America ballooned by 450 percent.[1] This phenomenal growth altered the balance of power when it came to covering high-profile crimes. Now viewers in California could learn about developments in New Jersey trials just as fast as someone living in Hoboken. No longer did the defendant have to contend with local hostility alone, now it came in the form of coast-to-coast loathing. The first, and arguably still the worst, example of a runaway, out-of-control media trampling a defendant's rights underfoot occurred in the mid-1950s, when an Ohio doctor found himself accused of murder. Before even a word of court-room testimony was heard, his name had been dragged through the mud, his private life scrutinized with Gestapo-like mercilessness, and he had been lynched in the court of public opinion. The venomous hate campaign waged against him owed more to an 18th-century witch hunt than it did to civilized standards of justice and fairness. Sam Sheppard's story sounded unlikely, but improbability does not necessarily imply guilt: life is strange and so, very often, is death.

This extraordinary saga had its beginnings on July 3, 1954, when Dr. Samuel Sheppard, an affluent 30-year-old osteopath, and his pregnant wife Marilyn invited their neighbors, the Ahearns, over for drinks at their home on the shores of Lake Erie, close to Cleveland. While the others watched TV, Sheppard dozed on the couch. Just after midnight the Ahearns left. Sheppard remained sleeping on the couch while Marilyn went to bed.

Some time later, according to his version of events, Sheppard heard a loud moan or scream. He rushed upstairs to the bedroom and saw "a white form"[2] standing beside the bed, leaning over Marilyn. Then everything went black. When he regained consciousness, Sheppard realized he had been clubbed on the neck. He stumbled across to the bed where Marilyn lay unmoving. A sudden noise sent him racing downstairs. By the rear door he spotted a tall man with bushy hair. He pursued the intruder onto the beach and tackled him from behind. During the struggle Sheppard blacked out again. This time, when he came around, he was partially immersed in the waters of Lake Erie. Groggily, he staggered back to the house and phoned for help.

Police found Marilyn's body lying in a pool of blood, her head and face smashed to a pulp. Downstairs, a writing desk had been ransacked and the contents of Sheppard's medical bag lay strewn across the floor. Apparently, someone had come to rob the house and ended up killing Marilyn.

Meantime, Sheppard had been whisked away by his two brothers to the hospital they owned jointly. It was this incident, more than any other, that unleashed the tidal wave of toxic press coverage that swamped this case. Circulation-hungry editors, spearheaded by Louis B. Seltzer, of the now defunct *Cleveland Press*, were convinced that the wealthy Sheppard Boys had closed ranks to protect their own. The accusations flew thick and fast.

The discovery at the house of a canvas bag, containing Sheppard's wristwatch, key chain and key, and a fraternity ring, gave rise to speculation that he had faked a robbery to conceal murder. But the clincher came with the revelation that Sheppard had been conducting an extramarital affair. Official suspicion soared exponentially. So did the media pressure. Finally, goaded beyond endurance by Seltzer's ravings—"Quit Stalling. Bring Him In!" screamed his July 30 editorial—detectives arrested Sheppard and took him into custody. Hundreds of people, newscasters, reporters, and photographers were milling round the jailhouse to record his arrival. That same night Sheppard was charged with murder.

The atrocities that Seltzer perpetrated on a local level were paralleled nationally by the influential radio reporter Walter Winchell. Winchell's attacks on Sheppard were relentless and would continue throughout Sheppard's trial. (Some jurors later admitted that, during the trial, they had listened to Winchell's broadcasts—which were littered with unsubstantiated rumors and flagrant fabrication—but claimed that they were unaffected by the allegations.) Television, too, added its weight to the army of prejudice arrayed against Sheppard. Night after night, news programs pumped pictures into homes across the nation, showing reporters baying for blood outside the jailhouse.

Amid unprecedented ballyhoo, on October 18 the state of Ohio opened its case against Sheppard. Judge Edward Blythin set the tone early. A candidate for reelection in the upcoming November ballot, he shamelessly curried favor with the press, issuing handwritten passes for the journalistic elite like Dorothy Kilgallen and Bob Considine, even providing them with their own special table at which to sit. By way of

Dr. Samuel Sheppard sits in a courtroom before the start of his trial in Cleveland, Ohio, in 1954. *AP Photo*

a bonus, he conveniently situated the table so that the reporters could eavesdrop on conversations between Sheppard and his counsel. Blythin presided over a madcap assembly of popping flash bulbs, vindictive reporters, and a hideous uproar that the Supreme Court would later deride as a "carnival atmosphere."[3] Even the jurors joined in, posing eagerly for the press photographs that would make them into local celebrities.

All this hoopla helped mask the fact that the state had a wafer-thin case against Sheppard. In the absence of any direct evidence against the defendant—other than that he was in the house when Marilyn was

(continues on page 92)

LYNCH LAW

Mob hysteria is almost impossible to control. Once it takes hold, it seems to have a life of its own. Just over four decades before the media lynching that Sam Sheppard endured, another man charged with murder also found himself having to battle not just the courts but also a viciously hostile local press. When the body of 13-year-old Mary Phagan was discovered in the early hours of April 27, 1913, at the Atlanta pencil factory where she worked, suspicion at first fell on the man who had found her, night watchman Newt Lee. Two scrawled notes, supposedly written by the dying Phagan, were found close to the body, and these accused an unnamed Negro of being her assailant. Lee, who was Black, was thrown into jail, but two days later the Jewish factory manager, Leo Frank, was also behind bars. Factory employees had claimed that Frank flirted with Mary to the point of scaring her and that he'd lured her to the factory late at night by deliberately withholding her pay. Frank's nervous, trembling manner under questioning did not impress detectives; they theorized that he had killed Phagan and then written the notes himself to throw investigators off the scent. At this time Atlanta was a hotbed of anti-Semitism and Frank's Jewishness was a recurring theme in press accounts of the crime.

At Frank's trial the main prosecution witness was Jim Conley, a large Black man who was the factory janitor. He told quite a story. Frank, he said, regularly seduced girls at the factory, while Conley acted as lookout. Mary Phagan was just his latest conquest. On the night of her death, Frank had confessed the killing to Conley and had dictated the two notes, which Conley took down, before Frank asked for Conley's help in moving the body. Then Frank had given Conley some cigarettes and told him to leave the factory. Try as they might—and some of the cross-examination was savagely racist in tone—the defense couldn't shake Conley's testimony. Nor could it get the jury to buy their argument that Conley was the real killer. On August 26 Frank was found guilty of murder and sentenced to hang. A series of appeals delayed the intended execution date until January 22, 1915, only for another motion to further postpone his date with the gallows. What the courts couldn't achieve, the outgoing governor of Georgia, John Slaton, did. Deeply troubled by the evidence in the case, and saying that it was "his duty,"[4] on June 21, 1915, Slaton commuted the sentence to life imprisonment and Frank was transferred to the Milledgeville Prison Farm, outside Macon.

Slaton's decision infuriated a local populist politician and publisher named Tom Watson. In a string of inflammatory articles, each more vitriolic than the last, he urged the citizens of Georgia to take the law into their hands. A wave of anti-Semitic rioting rocked Atlanta as Jewish homes and stores were attacked indiscriminately. But worse was to come. On August 16, 1915, a mob calling themselves the Knights of Mary Phagan stormed the Milledgeville Prison Farm, dragged Frank from his cell, and drove him back to Mary Phagan's hometown of Marietta. There, in the early hours of the following morning, Frank was hanged from the limb of a tree. He died still protesting his innocence.

The lynching was largely ignored by Georgia's citizens. Indeed, the murder of Mary Phagan acted as a rallying call for the Ku Klux Klan, which saw its membership expand on a rising tide of anti-Semitism. There was other fallout. In 1916 Frank's prosecutor, Hugh Dorsey, was elected governor of Georgia, and four years later, Tom Watson, became a senator.

In 1982 Alonzo Mann—who at the time of the murder had been a 13-year-old office boy at the pencil factory—broke a 69-year silence to say that on the night of the killing he had seen Conley, alone, dragging Mary Phagan's body to where it was found. Mann claimed that Conley had threatened to kill him if he said anything. Acting on this information, in 1986 the Georgia Board of Pardons agreed to grant Leo Frank a posthumous pardon based on the state's failure to protect him. It did not officially absolve him of the crime. As for Conley, there were reports that he had died in 1962, and there were rumors—nothing more—of a deathbed confession.

(continued from page 89)

killed—prosecutor John Mahon could only highlight the inconsistencies in Sheppard's story. Why was there no sand in his hair when he claimed to have been sprawled on the beach? Where was the T-shirt that he had been wearing? Had bloodstains received during the attack forced him to destroy it? And why would a burglar first take the belongings in the canvas bag and then ditch them? Besides which, said Mahon, the police could find no evidence that anyone had broken into the house. For motive, Mahon pointed to Sheppard's affair with Susan Hayes, a lab technician at the family hospital, as reason enough for him wanting to be rid of Marilyn.

Initially the lack of a murder weapon posed problems for the prosecution, but Cuyahoga County Coroner Samuel R. Gerber neatly circumvented this discrepancy by telling the court that a bloody imprint, found on the pillow beneath Marilyn's head, was made by a "two-bladed surgical instrument with teeth on the end of each blade,"[5] then hinted darkly that this was the missing weapon. Inexplicably, the defense left this vague assertion unchallenged, an omission that caused irreparable damage to their client's case. Nor did the defense explore Gerber's blatant antipathy toward the defendant. Around Cleveland, it was well known that Gerber hated the Sheppards. He had clashed with them previously over some medical matter and had come off worse in the exchange. In June 1954, according to an intern, Gerber had sworn to topple the entire Sheppard clan, saying, "I'm going to get them some day."[6]

Every point against Sheppard was hungrily reported, and sometimes distorted, by the media. Bob Considine, in a broadcast heard over station WHK in Cleveland, likened Sheppard "to a perjurer,"[7] and drew comparisons with Alger Hiss (the State Department official, who in 1950 had been convicted of perjury when accused of being a Soviet spy.) Again, several of the nonsequestered jurors admitting listening to Considine's overheated rhetoric. But Blythin refused to put a cap on the media coverage.

Susan Hayes, in her testimony, demurely cataloged a long-running romantic liaison and claimed that Sheppard was contemplating divorce. No salacious detail was spared. The reporters' pencils didn't stop scribbling. Apart from confirming that Sheppard had been unfaithful, Miss Hayes's testimony proved nothing. But the damage had been done. Sheppard, like many defendants before and since, ended up being tried more for his morals than for any crime. Defense attorney Fred Garmone's cross-examination of the witness was brief and went some way toward salvaging the loss. "Miss Hayes, in all your activities with Dr. Sheppard, were you always aware that he was a married man?"

"Yes,"[8] she whispered. With a telling look to the jury, Garmone announced that he had no more questions.

Arguably, the most potent prosecution witness was Judge Blythin. His antipathy toward the defendant was plain and unvarnished. Early in the trial he had remarked to Dorothy Kilgallen: "[Sheppard's] as guilty as hell. There's no question about it,"[9] and throughout the proceedings he had hectored and hamstrung the defense at every turn. Such animosity from the bench utterly demolished Sheppard's last hope of receiving a fair trial. His own appearance on the stand was largely irrelevant. He performed well, but not well enough to overcome the poisonous courtroom atmosphere.

Jury deliberations lasted four days—almost within earshot of a temporary TV studio that had been set up in an adjacent room—and resulted in a verdict of guilty of second-degree murder. (A rumor that some jurors were unwilling to commit a doctor to the electric chair for first-degree murder and might therefore acquit Sheppard, had obliged Judge Blythin to make available the possibility of conviction for the lesser charge of second-degree murder.) Blythin pronounced sentence: "It is now the judgment of this court that you be taken to the Ohio Penitentiary, there to remain for the rest of your natural life."[10]

While Cleveland's newspapers whooped their delight, a tiny group of out-of-town journalists was utterly dismayed by the verdict. The way they saw and reported it, Sheppard had been convicted for adultery, nothing more. Thanks largely to their well-documented outrage, Sheppard's name stayed in the public arena. Then, in 1963, something remarkable happened—a hugely successful TV series called *The Fugitive* began to air. Although the producers later denied it, many felt that it had been based on the Sheppard case. Each week millions tuned in to watch the patently innocent and marvelously angst-ridden Dr. Richard

Reporters busy themselves in the press room at the Cleveland Criminal Courts Building during Samuel Sheppard's murder trial in 1954. The media's unfair treatment of Sheppard led to a retrial and his eventual acquittal in 1966. *Bettmann/Corbis*

Kimble, as he battled all odds to track down the elusive "one-armed man" who had really killed his wife. For some impressionable viewers, Kimble and Sheppard became interchangeable players in the same story. As the viewing figures soared, so did concerns about the unfairness of Sam Sheppard's trial.

Someone already deeply committed to the mission of getting Sheppard a new trial was the flamboyant attorney F. Lee Bailey. Back in November 1961, while still a 29-year-old newcomer, Bailey had taken up the fight on Sheppard's behalf and, in the years that followed, he had filed a stream of motions for a retrial, only to see every one rejected. His frustration built until March 1964 when, by chance, Bailey attended a literary dinner. Among the other guests was Dorothy Kilgallen, and she happened to repeat Judge Blythin's off-the-record remark made to her during the trial. Bailey couldn't believe his ears: This was legal

THE DIGITAL REVOLUTION

The Internet has changed the way people live. And it also had an enormous impact on the way the courts conduct business. This is especially true when considering *sub judice*, the legal requirement stating that once a legal case is underway then all media opinion about that case is barred until a verdict is delivered. Most Western countries adhere strictly to this concept; America does not. Given the limitless reach of the Internet, the concept of *sub judice* is looking more threatened. Throughout much of the 20th century, most people received their news via the radio, television, or newspaper, and reached their conclusions accordingly. Normally these conclusions were discussed with just a few close friends, but nowadays the Internet has opened up every crime case to worldwide discussion. Opinions, often based on the skimpiest evidence—and occasionally on no evidence at all—are tossed into the ether like cyber confetti. Many of these emanate from blogs and Web sites that deal with nothing except the latest major crime cases. Some go to great lengths to check their facts and present a balanced view; others verge on the hysterical. What they both share is a potentially global audience. And it is from these readers that jurors are chosen.

At one time, especially in sensational cases, it was customary for defense lawyers to apply for a change of trial venue, on grounds that prejudicial local media coverage had made it impossible for the defendant to get a fair trial in the district where the crime occurred. Sometimes this was granted; mostly it was denied. Modern communication technology has rendered that option almost redundant. Because the details of all high-profile crimes are now available to anyone with a computer and an Internet connection, shifting a trial from, say, Amarillo, Texas, more than 800 miles south to Brownsville is increasingly unlikely to have any bearing on the outcome. In cyberspace distance is meaningless and there is no evidence that it dilutes prejudice or bias.

dynamite. If he could demonstrate blatant judicial prejudice then it would constitute clear grounds for a new trial.

The courts agreed. Just four months later Sheppard was freed on bail by federal District Judge Carl A. Weinman. "If ever there was a trial by newspaper, this is a perfect example,"[11] declared Weinman. After lambasting the combined Cleveland media, Weinman saved most of his barbs for the now dead Blythin. Because of the judge's biased and lax control, Sheppard was subjected to a trial that ". . . fell far below the minimum requirements for due process."[12]

The following year Bailey argued his case before the Supreme Court, claiming that Blythin's conduct and blatant prejudice meant that the trial had been conducted in a manner unbecoming a legal action. The Court agreed. On June 6, 1965, they handed down their landmark decision that Sheppard's 1954 conviction be set aside, because Judge Blythin "did not fulfill his duty to protect Sheppard from the inherently prejudicial publicity which saturated the community and to control disruptive influences in the courtroom."[13]

Stubborn to the end, Ohio tried Sheppard again. Media interest remained high but this time was kept in check when the trial opened on October 24, 1966, before Judge Francis J. Talty. Prosecutor John Corrigan led witnesses through essentially the same story that they had told over a decade earlier, but they now faced a defense attorney at the peak of his powers. Bailey demolished them, particularly Coroner Gerber. Referring to the elusive "surgical instrument," Gerber foolishly announced that he had spent the last 12 years hunting for just such an item "all over the United States."

Bailey pounced. "Tell us what you found?"

Too late, Gerber realized that he had talked himself into a trap. "I didn't find one,"[14] he muttered feebly. Gerber's lame response provided the catalyst for Bailey to scathingly dismiss the prosecution's case as "ten pounds of hogwash in a five pound bag."[15]

On December 16, 1966, the jury took fewer than 12 hours to return a verdict of not guilty: Sam Sheppard's ordeal was over. But liberty proved tragically brief. His health deteriorated quickly, hastened by an increasing addiction to vodka and painkillers. Sheppard died on April 6, 1970, at the age of 46.

Journalistic irresponsibility, kindled by greedy editors, stole a decade of freedom from Sam Sheppard and probably sent him to an early grave. Trial by media is still a problem, just as potent, just as pernicious as ever. It refuses to go away. And so does the Sheppard saga. In the 1990s Sheppard's son, Sam Reese Sheppard, went head to head with the state of Ohio, determined to prove that a Bay Village handyman named Richard Eberling had been the real killer. In doing so, Sheppard hoped to clear his father's name once and for all.

Because this was a civil action, the eight-member jury would reach their decision on the **preponderance of the evidence**, rather than the more stringent requirements of a criminal trial, which requires guilt to be established "beyond a reasonable doubt." On balance this favored the **plaintiffs**: They had to demonstrate only that Sam Sheppard had probably not killed his wife. However, as any defense lawyer knows, proving innocence can often be far tougher than establishing guilt.

And so it proved. On April 12, 2000, a Cleveland jury found for the state of Ohio. In effect they were saying that Sam Sheppard was "not innocent" of his wife's murder. It remains an appropriately ambiguous verdict for this most baffling of crimes, for despite all the searing doubts and suspicion, there wasn't a scintilla of hard evidence to prove that Sam Sheppard killed his wife in 1954. There still isn't.

8

The Appeal
Process

In the United States, every criminal conviction can be appealed and most are. This right is entirely one-sided, as the state or prosecution has no such right of appeal against a jury or bench verdict of acquittal in a criminal case. The idea is to give the prisoner the greatest possible chance to prove his or her innocence. As noble as this sounds, it does cause problems. Over the centuries the United States has evolved the most complex, lengthy, and, at times, frustrating appeals systems in the world. This is especially true in death penalty cases, where the appeals can drag on for decades. Supporters of the drawn-out process claim, with some justification, that only by exploring every legal avenue is it possible to arrive at justice. They highlight the 17 death row inmates subsequently exonerated by fresh DNA evidence.[1] Opponents argue, with equal validity, that most appeals are frivolous, engineered by ideologically motivated attorneys prepared to use every stalling device available to advance their own agenda, which is the abolition of capital punishment. Striking a balance between the rights of the individual and the wishes of the majority of society is never easy. And what about the rights of victim's relatives? What part—if any—should they play in the appeal process? Usually, theirs are the silent voices. But there are times when everybody needs to stand up and be counted.

In the spring of 1973 Carl Isaacs was 19 years old, on the run, and just about to commit one of the worst crimes in living memory. On May 5 he had escaped from Poplar Hill Correctional Camp, a minimum security facility near Salisbury, Maryland. With him were his half-brother Wayne Coleman, 26, and a friend, George Dungee, 35. Once free, they were joined by Carl's 16-year-old brother, Billy, who had just absconded from the Victor Cullen School for boys, in Sabillasville, Maryland. The gang had cooked up a plan to head for Florida. The afternoon of May 14, 1973, found the fugitives in Donalsonville, Georgia, just a few miles from the Florida state line. Their car was almost out of gas. Creeping along to save fuel, they spotted what looked like a gas pump behind a mobile home. It turned out that they were mistaken, there was no pump. But the trailer home was empty and so they decided to ransack it.

While Dungee remained in the car, Carl Isaacs and Coleman entered the mobile home. They were still inside when Billy Isaacs warned them that two men were approaching in a jeep. Jerry Alday, 35, the owner of the trailer home, and his 62-year-old father, Ned, pulled in behind the trailer, oblivious to the fact that it was being burglarized. The first they knew that something was wrong came when Carl Isaacs stepped out and ordered them inside at gunpoint. Their pockets were emptied, and then Jerry Alday was taken into the south bedroom of the trailer while Ned was taken to the north bedroom. Without any warning, Carl Isaacs shot and killed Jerry Alday, pumping four bullets into his head. Then he and Coleman opened fire on Ned. The medical examiner found that he'd received seven gunshots to the head.

The calamities for the Alday family continued to mount. A short while later, Jerry's brother, Jimmy Alday, 25, drove up on a tractor, walked to the back of the trailer and knocked on the door. Coleman answered the door, "stuck a pistol up in the guy's face,"[2] and hustled him inside. Jimmy was taken into the living room, his pockets were emptied, and he was forced to lie on the couch. Moments later he was dead, shot in the back of the head by Carl Isaacs. Isaacs then hurried outside to move the tractor, which was parked in front of their car. At that moment, Jerry's wife, Mary, 25, drove up. Carl Isaacs waited until she entered the trailer, and then jumped her. "She was crying, sort of like whimpering," said Billy Isaacs later. "Carl told her to shut up."[3] Mrs. Alday was forced into the kitchen, where her purse was rifled. It contained her car keys and a dollar bill. Just then a pickup truck drew up outside. Coleman and Dungee shoved Mary into the bathroom, while Carl and Billy Isaacs went outside to confront the newcomers. Another of Jerry's brothers, Chester, 32, and his 56-year-old uncle, Aubrey Alday, could only stare disbelievingly as they were herded into the trailer at gunpoint. Once inside, Aubrey was taken to the south bedroom where Carl Isaacs shot and killed him, while Chester Alday was taken to the north bedroom and killed by Coleman. All the victims had been shot from one to seven times in the back of the head. Coleman and Carl Isaacs then proceeded to rape Mary Alday on her kitchen table.

Some time later, they drove her to a heavily wooded area some six miles away where Mary Alday was first tortured, then raped again. Her agony ended when Dungee shot her twice, once in the head and again in the torso. They dumped her naked body in the woods, along with their own car. Then the four men took off in Mary's car, which they later abandoned in Alabama. There they stole another car and drove north. On May 18 the Isaacs brothers and Coleman were arrested in Welch, West Virginia. Dungee had been apprehended one day earlier, after the four men had fled on foot from a roadblock. Their guilt was not in question. Their fingerprints were all over the Alday house; they were in possession of three handguns later identified as the murder weapons, and they had property belonging to the victims.

Prosecutors called the slayings the most gruesome murders in the state's history, and local feelings ran high when Carl Isaacs stood trial. He was the first to be tried. He sat and grimaced as his brother, who'd plea bargained his way to a 40-year sentence, described in chilling detail how the Aldays had been systematically slaughtered. On January 3, 1974, Isaacs was convicted and sentenced to death. One Alday family member was heard to murmur, "So far, so good."[4] when the punishment was handed down. Doubtless that same person felt that some kind of closure had been achieved when, later that same year, Coleman and Dungee were also condemned to death. But, in reality, the battle had only just begun.

The first hurdle to overcome was constitutional. The death sentences imposed on Isaacs and his cohorts came two years after *Furman v. Georgia*, 408 U.S. 238 (1972), in which the Supreme Court struck down Georgia's capital punishment statute, ruling that the system's

Law-enforcement officials stand outside the home of Mary Alday and her husband Jerry, who were killed along with four other family members on May 14, 1973. *AP Photo*

arbitrary and often disproportionate nature constituted cruel and unusual punishment. The court's decision forced states to rethink the wording of their statutes for capital offenses, to ensure that the death penalty would not be imposed in a discriminatory manner. Such a ruling effectively dumped Isaacs into a kind of no-man's-land. Was he under a death sentence or not? Across America, a moratorium was called on executions. Some states automatically commuted all death sentences; others, including Georgia, kept their death row inmates in legal limbo while legislators reworded the capital punishment statutes. And then it was back to the Supreme Court. In 1976 the court revisited the issue, in *Gregg v. Georgia*, 428 U.S. 153, and this time it found that the state's revised penalty statutes were constitutional. This decision, in tandem with other Supreme Court decisions, effectively reinstated capital punishment in the United States. In the case of Isaacs, Coleman, and Dungee it meant that, once again, they were facing a date with the electric chair.

In the United States, all death penalty convictions are automatically appealed, and this is what leads to the often quite extraordinary amount of time that elapses between sentencing and execution. However, not all prisoners are prepared to countenance the protracted ordeal. For instance, Joe F. Gonzales, who arrived on the Texas death row on

THE COST OF CAPITAL PUNISHMENT

There is one element in the hotly contested death penalty debate on which all sides are agreed: Capital punishment is very expensive. At every stage of the process, from trial, to incarceration, to appeals, costs soar way beyond what is standard in noncapital cases. Nobody knows the exact cost of executing an individual, but estimates range from $1.7 million to $3 million. Abolitionists argue that it would be much more cost-effective to simply incarcerate someone for life without the possibility of parole. In 2008 the state of California, which has the most densely populated death row in the nation, published a report that attempted to put some flesh on this claim. From the data studied it concluded, "The additional cost of confining an inmate to death row, as compared to the maximum security prisons where those sentenced to life without the possibility of parole ordinarily serve their sentences, is $90,000 per year per inmate. With California's current death row population of 670, that accounts for $63.3 million annually."[5] The report also conservatively estimated the total cost of the death penalty at $137 million per year.

New Jersey was another state struggling to justify the crippling costs of the death penalty. A 2005 report revealed that, since the reinstatement of capital punishment in 1982, New Jersey taxpayers had shelled out $253.3 million dollars

January 10, 1996, chose to waive his right to appeals, making it quite clear that he wanted nothing to interfere with what he regarded as his inevitable fate. On September 18, after just 252 days on death row, he was executed by lethal injection.

This is very much the exception. Death row inmates in the United States typically spend more than a decade awaiting execution. Supreme Court justices Stephen Breyer and John Paul Stephens have questioned

to pursue capital cases. That money bought them 197 capital trials, 60 death penalty convictions, 50 reversals of conviction, and not a single execution. A quarter of a billion dollars buys an awful lot of law enforcement capacity in the way of extra police officers, as well as ensuring that the really bad guys are locked away for ever. Little wonder, then, that in December 2007, Governor Jon Corzine signed a bill abolishing the state's death penalty.

On March 16, 2009, New Mexico also joined the abolitionist states. Other states are considering the financial sense of maintaining a penalty that costs so much to administer and achieves so little in return.

The criminal justice system does not operate in a vacuum. It, too, has been badly hit by the financial crisis that struck in 2008. As tax revenues sink, and legislators look for ways to tighten the purse strings, it is likely that the abolitionist cause will gain converts, however reluctant some of these might be. Much more predictable is the certainty that pro-death penalty campaigners will fight tooth and nail to keep capital punishment on the statute book. They blame the high costs on conniving lawyers, and a legal system that permits so many appeals. The solution, they say, is to limit any prisoner to just one appeal. If that fails, it's time to set an execution date. And that's the cheapest part of the process. In Texas, which has the busiest death chamber in the nation—18 executions in 2008—the cocktail of drugs that goes into its lethal injection costs just $86.08.

OVERTURNING THE VERDICT

The courts don't always get it right. In the rush to condemn the United States legal system for its perceived tardiness, many forget that justice isn't just about convicting the guilty, it's also about making sure the innocent walk free. In 1977 Ohio-born Randall Dale Adams, 27, was charged with murdering a Dallas, Texas, police officer, Robert Woods. Much of the prosecution's case centered around the testimony of David Harris, 16, who was arrested three weeks after the shooting, having bragged of killing an officer in Dallas. (He later led the police to a swamp, where they recovered the murder weapon.) Harris admitted to having been present at the shooting, but claimed that Adams had pulled the trigger. Adams was charged with murder. At the trial, Adams, who had hitched a ride with Harris, insisted that he had left the car two hours before the fatal incident. With the testimony seemingly deadlocked, at the 11th hour the prosecution produced three surprise witnesses who claimed to have seen Adams at the crime scene. As a result of this testimony, Adams was convicted and sentenced to death.

The fight continued. In June 1980 the Supreme Court stayed Adams' impending execution on grounds of improper

the constitutionality of such delays, but others argue that this legal foot-dragging is integral to the United States legal process, helping to significantly reduce the risk of a miscarriage of justice.

Isaacs was certainly in no rush to reach the death chamber. Nor were Coleman and Dungee. All three appealed their convictions. An appeal is not a retrial of the case, but an examination of the trial record to ensure that proceedings were conducted in a fair manner. Often trial lawyers don't conduct appeals. This is the province of the specialist. Attorneys, experienced in appeal law, will scour the trial transcripts, hunting for any hint of error. It might hinge upon the proficiency or otherwise of defense counsel; the admissibility of evidence; an alleged misdirection of the jury from the bench; anything that might be considered prejudicial to the defendant's right to a fair trial.

jury selection. Dallas prosecutors, fearing that this might lead to a retrial, hurriedly advised the governor that Adams' sentence be commuted to life imprisonment. This, they felt, resolved the situation.

But in 1985, Harris, who by now was on death row for another killing, began dropping hints that his testimony against Adams had resulted from coaching by ambitious conviction-hungry prosecutors. In a series of taped interviews Harris obliquely admitted that he had shot Woods. The three eyewitnesses also admitted that their evidence had been compromised.

Suspicions of prosecutorial malfeasance kept the case alive and, in 1989, led an appeals court to order Adams' release on grounds that the state had deliberately withheld evidence from the defense. While refusing to admit any error, prosecutors declined to retry Adams and he was freed. Harris was never tried for the murder of Officer Woods, and on June 30, 2004, he was executed for the other murder.

In 1988 Errol Morris' Oscar-nominated docudrama, *The Thin Blue Line*, brought the name of Randall Adams to national prominence. A searching examination of Dallas justice, it also highlighted the absolute need for a comprehensive and rigorous appeals system.

If a perceived error is found, it makes its way into a brief that is ultimately heard by the appeal court. The judges are not just looking for mistakes, but for the number and the gravity of those mistakes. If the appeal court agrees that errors have been made, it then has to decide what impact—if any—these mistakes might have had on the outcome of the trial. If sufficient substantive errors are uncovered, the conviction will, most likely, be overturned. This is not common. Some studies claim that over 90 percent of such appeals in criminal cases fail.

Another ground for appeal in a criminal trial—used almost exclusively in high-profile cases—is the charge that sensational local media coverage violated the defendant's rights to a fair trial, and that the judge should have ordered a change of venue. This was the argument, after 11 years of failed appeals, that lawyers for Isaacs, Dungee and Coleman took to the United States Court of Appeals for the Eleventh Circuit in 1985. Attached to the brief was a 100-page summary of news reports about the Alday murders that, the brief claimed, made it impossible for the three to receive fair trials in Seminole County, Georgia, where the killings occurred. On December 9, 1985, the three-judge panel issued its decision. In a 128-page opinion, one of the longest in the history of the appeals court for the Eleventh Circuit, the judges wrote that even "an obviously guilty defendant"[6] has the right to a fair trial. They continued, "Inflammatory and prejudicial pretrial publicity so pervaded the community as to render virtually impossible a fair trial before an impartial jury."[7] They noted the comments of the Seminole County sheriff who was quoted as saying before the trial, "If I had my way about it, I'd have me a large oven and I'd precook them for several days."[8] Such an atmosphere made it inconceivable to think that the defendants "received an impartial assessment."[9] Accordingly, all three convictions were overturned and retrials were ordered.

The court's decision outraged the citizens of Seminole County. They raised a petition with 100,000 signatures that demanded the impeachment of the three federal judges who'd allowed the appeal. Most unusually, this demand reached as far as Washington, D.C., and the House Judiciary Committee. On October 25, 1986, it categorically refused to commence impeachment proceedings against Frank M. Johnson Jr., R. Lanier Anderson III, and Thomas A. Clark, ruling explicitly for the first time that a judge cannot be subjected to impeachment for a judicial decision, even if it's subsequently shown to be erroneous.

Once again Isaacs was the first to be tried, this time in Houston County, Georgia. On January 25, 1988, the jury, which this time listened to a tape made after the first trial, on which Isaacs could be heard confessing the crimes, took two hours and 10 minutes to find Isaacs guilty on six counts of murder. Five days later, he was again sentenced to death. Later that same year, Coleman and Dungee stood trial. Both were convicted, but this time both were spared the death penalty. In Coleman's case, the jury deadlocked over the sentence and he received life imprisonment. Because Dungee pleaded guilty, and because there was evidence to show that Dungee was mentally retarded, he too was imprisoned for life.

Carl Isaacs was finally given a lethal injection on May 5, 2003, 30 years after orchestrating the slaughter of six members of the Alday family. *AP Photo/Georgia Department of Corrections*

This just left Isaacs—widely considered to be the ringleader—to face the full wrath of the law. He wasn't about to give up without a struggle. The appeals continued to be filed and were routinely rejected. For the Alday family members, frustration slowly turned to fury. Making it worse, in their eyes, was the way that they were kept in the dark at each step of the way. Every new development, every Byzantine twist, filtered down to them via the media. At no time did the judicial system keep them apprised of what was happening.

Each passing year only added to their anger. In 1994 another kick in the belly came with news that Billy Isaacs, after serving 20 years, had been granted parole. More than two decades of legal heel-dragging took a terrible toll on the Alday family. Some of their resentment switched away from Isaacs and onto the legal system that was keeping him alive and them in the dark. They demanded a better deal. Eventually their outrage reached all the way to the state capital. On February 8, 2002, the House unanimously passed House Bill 1070, a bill ordering the attorney general that, in a case in which the accused is convicted of a capital offense, the victim's family should be notified at least twice per year regarding legal proceedings, if they so desire, until the accused dies.

A year earlier, Isaacs had again appealed to the Eleventh U.S. Circuit Court of Appeals, claiming his rights were violated 32 times during his retrial. This time the court refused his appeal and upheld his death sentence, a decision later endorsed by the United States Supreme Court.

Time finally ran out for Carl Isaacs on May 5, 2003, when he was given a lethal injection at the state prison in Jackson. At the time of his execution, Isaacs had spent more time on death row—30 years and 4 months—than any other inmate in America. (That dubious distinction has now passed to Florida's Gary Alvord, who was sentenced to death on April 9, 1974, and, at the time of writing, is still on death row.)

Outside the prison at the appointed hour stood a 60-strong gathering of people who had made the 200 mile trip from Donalsville to Jackson. Inside, for the first time in Georgia history, three relatives of the victims were permitted to witness the execution. As the law had finally recognized they had rights, too.

Endnotes

Introduction
1. *State v. Hall*, 187 So. 2d 861 (1966).

Chapter 1
1. "Assize of Clarendon." *Encyclopedia Britannica*, 2001 (CD ROM)
2. Douglas Linder, "Examination of Tituba," Famous Trials/University of Missouri Kansas City School of Law, http://www.law.umkc.edu/faculty/projects/ftrials/salem/ASA_TITX.HTM (Accessed March 27, 2009).
3. *Ibid*.
4. Douglas Linder, "The Witchcraft Trials in Salem," Famous Trials/University of Missouri Kansas City School of Law, http://www.law.umkc.edu/faculty/projects/ftrials/salem/SAL_ACCT.HTM (Accessed March 27, 2009).
5. U.S. Census Bureau, "1800–1990: Changes in Urban/Rural U.S. Population," ElderWeb, http://www.elderweb.com/home/node/2836 (Accessed March 30, 2009).
6. *Los Angeles Times*, "Editorial: Spector—And Expert Witnesses—On Trial," *LATimes.com*, http://www.latimes.com/news/opinion/la-ed-witness30-2009-mar30,0,7983947.story (Accessed March 30, 2009).

7. Steven Mikulan, "Accidental Suicide?" *LAWeekly.com*, http://www.laweekly.com/2009-04-02/columns/accidental-suicide-new-involuntary-manslaughter-option-in-phil-spector-murder-retrial (Accessed April 25, 2009).

Chapter 2
1. *Arizona v. Miranda*, 98 Ariz. 18; 401 P.2d 721 (1965).
2. *Ibid*.
3. *Ibid*.
4. *Ibid*.
5. *Gideon v. Wainwright*, 372 U.S. 335 (1963).

Chapter 3
1. "F.B.I. Inquiry Ordered," *New York Times*, June 23, 1964.
2. Jerry W. DeLaughter, "Defense Mounts Case," *Christian Science Monitor*, October 18, 1967.
3. "It May Give a New Face to Justice in the South," *New York Times*, October 22, 1967.
4. Federal Bureau of Investigation, "Crime in the United States, by Community Type, 2005," http://www.fbi.gov/ucr/cius2008/data/table_02.html (Accessed October 27, 2009).
5. Walter Rugaber, "All-White Jury Picked," *New York Times*, October 10, 1967.

6. Walter Rugaber, "Informer Links Klan to Rights Slaying," *New York Times*, October 12, 1967.

7. *Ibid.*

8. Walter Rugaber, "Witness Tells of Role in Slaying of Rights Workers," *New York Times*, October 13, 1967.

9. Jack Nelson, "Killings Pleased Klan," *Washington Post*, October, 13, 1967.

10. *Ibid.*

11. *Ibid.*

12. "Testimony of Charles Johnson," Famous Trials/University of Missouri Kansas City School of Law, http://www.law.umkc.edu/faculty/projects/ftrials/price&bowers/Johnson.html (Accessed March 26, 2009).

13. Walter Rugaber, "All-White Jury Picked," *New York Times*, October 10, 1967.

14. Walter Rugaber, "Trial of 18 Charged with Conspiracy," *New York Times*, October 19, 1967.

15. "Character Witnesses Called," *Washington Post*, October 17, 1967.

16. Walter Rugaber, "Defense Calls Two Negroes as Character Witnesses," *New York Times*, October 17, 1967.

17. Walter Rugaber, "Trial of 18 Charged with Conspiracy," *New York Times*, October 19, 1967.

18. "Closing Argument by Mr. Doar," Famous Trials/University of Missouri Kansas City School of Law, http://www.law.umkc.edu/faculty/projects/ftrials/price&bowers/doarclose.htm (Accessed March 26, 2009).

19. *Ibid.*

20. Walter Rugaber, "Trial of 18 Charged with Conspiracy," *New York Times*, October 19, 1967.

21. "Closing Argument by Mr. Doar," Famous Trials/University of Missouri Kansas City School of Law, http://www.law.umkc.edu/faculty/projects/ftrials/price&bowers/doarclose.htm (Accessed March 26, 2009).

22. Ibid.

23. Walter Rugaber, "Trial of 18 Charged with Conspiracy," *New York Times*, October 19, 1967.

24. "All-White Jury Will Try 18 In Rights Killings," *Washington Post*, October 10, 1967.

Chapter 4

1. "Attorney Hunter Assault," *The San Francisco Call*, May 20, 1892. http://chroniclingamerica.loc.gov/lccn/sn94052989/1892-05-22/ed-1/seq-10 (Accessed October 27, 2009)

2. "Jay E. Hunter Fatally Shot," *The San Francisco Call*, February 19, 1989. http://chroniclingamerica.loc.gov/lccn/sn85066387/1899-02-19/ed-1/seq-1/ (Accessed October 27, 2009)

3. John H. Morrow Jr., and Earl Rogers Jr., eds., "A Yankee Ace in the RAF," University Press of Kansas, http://www.kansaspress.ku.edu/moryan.html (Accessed April 27, 2009).

4. Alfred Cohn and Joe Chisholm, *Take the Witness* (New York: Frederick A. Stokes Co., 1934), 26.

5. *Ibid.*

6. *Ibid, 28.*

7. *Ibid, 59.*

8. Francis Wellman, *The Art of Cross Examination*, (New York: Touchstone, 1997), 130.

Chapter 5

1. Gregory E. Mize, Paula Hannaford-Agor, and Nicole L. Waters, "The State of the States Survey of Jury Improvement Efforts," National Center for State Courts/State Justice Institute, http://www.ncsconline.org/D_Research/cjs/pdf/SOSCompendiumFinal.pdf (Accessed October 9, 2009)

2. *People v. Goetz*, 68 N.Y.2d 96; 497 N.E.2d 41; 506 N.Y.S.2d 18 (1986).

3. Margot Hornblower, "Jury Refuses to Indict Goetz for Attempted Murder," *Washington Post*, January 25, 1985.

4. Margot Hornblower, "Selection Begins for Goetz Jury," *Washington Post*, March 24, 1987.

5. Kirk Johnson, "Goetz Called a Powder Keg by Prosecutor," *New York Times*, April 28, 1987.

6. Edward W. Knappman, ed., *Great American Trials* (Detroit: Visible Ink, 1994), 751.

7. Kirk Johnson, "Goetz Called a Powder Keg by Prosecutor," *New York Times*, April 28, 1987.

8. Margot Hornblower, "'Subway Vigilante' Goetz Goes on Trial in N.Y.," *Washington Post*, April 28, 1987.

9. Edward W. Knappman, ed., *Great American Trials* (Detroit: Visible Ink, 1994), 751.

10. *Ibid*.

11. *Ibid*.

12. *People v. Goetz*, 68 N.Y.2d 96; 497 N.E.2d 41; 506 N.Y.S.2d 18 (1986).

13. "You Have to Think in a Cold-Blooded Way," *New York Times*, April 30, 1987.

14. George James, "In a Reversal, Youth Shot by Goetz Agrees to Testify for Prosecution," *New York Times*, May 16, 1987.

15. Kirk Johnson, "Goetz Jury Hears Charge by Judge and Deliberates," *New York Times*, June 13, 1987.

16. David E. Pitt, "Goetz Jurors Found Both Sides' Evidence Difficult to Accept," *New York Times*, June 17, 1987.

17. Margot Hornblower, "Jury Exonerates Goetz in 4 Subway Shootings," *Washington Post*, June 17, 1987.

18. David E. Pitt, "Goetz Jurors Found Both Sides' Evidence Difficult to Accept," *New York Times*, June 17, 1987.

19. *Ibid*.

Chapter 6

1. Roger Kahn, "Case of the Dead Bookie," *Saturday Evening Post* 238, 5 (March 13, 1965), 39.

2. *Ibid*, 38.

3. *Ibid*, 43.

4. Edith Evans Asbury, "Fein Sentencing Scheduled January 6," *New York Times*, November 26, 1964.

5. Roger Kahn, "Case of the Dead Bookie," *Saturday Evening Post* 238, 5 (March 13, 1965), 39.

6. Edith Evans Asbury, "Prostitute Tells of Loan to Fein," *New York Times*, November 10, 1964.

7. Roger Kahn, "Case of the Dead Bookie," *Saturday Evening Post* 238, 5 (March 13, 1965), 35.

8. *Time*, "The Madam's Mark," *Time.com* (November 20, 1964), http://www.time.com/time/magazine/

article/0,9171,830783,00.html (Accessed October 9, 2009).

9. *Ibid.*

10. *Ibid.*

11. *Ibid.*

12. Edward W. Knappman, ed., *Great American Trials* (Detroit: Visible Ink, 1994), 398.

13. *Time*, "Á Matter of Degree," *Time. com* (December 4, 1964), http:// www.time.com/time/magazine/ article/0,9171,830864,00.htm (Accessed October 9, 2009).

14. Edith Evans Asbury, "Mrs. Fein Called as Final Witness." *New York Times*, November 21, 1964.

15. Edith Evans Asbury, "Fein Murder Case Goes to the Jury," *New York Times*, November 24, 1964.

16. *People v. Fein,* 18 N.Y.2d 162; 219 N.E.2d 274; 272 N.Y.S.2d 753 (1966).

17. Edith Evans Asbury, "Fein Murder Case Goes to the Jury," *New York Times*, November 24, 1964.

Chapter 7

1. "Statistics on Radio and Television 1950–1960," UNESCO, http://unesdoc.unesco.org/ images/0003/000337/033739eo.pdf (Accessed March 17, 2009).

2. F. Lee Bailey and Harvey Aronson, *The Defense Never Rests*, (New York: Stein & Day, 1971), 70.

3. "Gov. Slaton's Statement," *New York Times*, June 22, 1915.

4. *Sheppard v. Maxwell,* 384 U.S. 333, 358 (1964) (U.S. Supreme Court).

5. Dorothy Kilgallen, *Murder One* (New York: Random House, 1967), 260.

6. John F. Hagan, and James Ewinger, "Coroner's 1966 Testimony Is Read in Sheppard Trial," *Plain Dealer*, March 7, 2000.

7. "Excerpts from High Court Ruling in Sheppard Case," *New York Times*, June 7, 1966.

8. Douglas Lindner, "The State of Ohio versus Sam Sheppard— October 18, 1954," Famous Trials/ University of Missouri Kansas City School of Law http://www.law. umkc.edu/faculty/projects/ftrials/ sheppard/1954TrialAccount.htm (Accessed March 17, 2009).

9. Dorothy Kilgallen, *Murder One*, (New York: Random House, 1967), 302.

10. Douglas Lindner, "The State of Ohio versus Sam Sheppard— October 18, 1954," Famous Trials/ University of Missouri Kansas City School of Law http://www.law. umkc.edu/faculty/projects/ftrials/ sheppard/1954TrialAccount.htm (Accessed March 17, 2009).

11. "U.S. Judge Orders Sheppard's Release," *New York Times*, July 16, 1964.

12. *Ibid.*

13. *Sheppard v. Maxwell,* 384 U.S. 333, 358 (1964) (U.S. Supreme Court).

14. F. Lee Bailey, and Harvey Aronson, *The Defense Never Rests*, (New York: Stein & Day, 1971), 109.

15. Marjorie Cohn, and David Dow, *Cameras in the Courtroom* (Lanham, Maryland: Rowman & Littlefield, 1998), 132.

Chapter 8

1. The Innocence Project, "Facts on Post-Conviction DNA Exonerations," Innocence Project.org http://www.innocenceproject.org/ Content/351.php (Accessed October 9, 2009).

2. *Isaacs v. State,* 259 Ga. 717; 386 S.E.2d 316 (1989).

3. "Brother Killed 5, Youth Testifies," *New York Times,* January 3, 1974.

4. "Jury Convict Youth of Killing a Family of Six in Georgia," *New York Times,* January 4, 1974.

5. Gerald Uelmen, ed., *California Commission for the Fair Administration of Justice, Final Report,* http://ccfaj.org/documents/ CCFAJFinalReport.pdf. (Posted June 30, 2008), 141.

6. "Convictions Overturned in Georgia Killing of 6," *New York Times,* December 11, 1985.

7. Jerry Schwartz, "Man Convicted Again in Killing of Georgia Family," *New York Times,* January 26, 1988.

8. *Ibid.*

9. *Ibid.*

Glossary

anthropology   The study of humankind

double jeopardy   A bar against double prosecution for the same offense. In practice, it means that if someone has been found innocent of a crime, even if conclusive evidence of guilt subsequently comes to light, that person is immune to prosecution for that offense

due process   A guarantee of judicial fairness to someone when the state deprives an individual of liberty or property

Fifth Amendment   A constitutionally mandated right against self-incrimination

fruit of the poisoned tree   In criminal law, the doctrine that evidence discovered due to information found through illegal search or other unconstitutional means (such as a forced confession) may not be introduced by a prosecutor

habeas corpus   A procedure for a judicial ruling on the legality of an individual's custody

impeachment   Criminal proceeding against a public official accused of wrong-doing while in office

incommunicado   Without access to any form of communication

moratorium   A suspension of activity, or a waiting period, set by an authority

panhandling   Begging

petit jury   An ordinary trial jury of 12 (usually) persons, as distinct from a grand jury of up to 23 persons

pettifogger   One given to quibbling over trifles

plaintiff   A person who initiates a lawsuit, seeking a remedy for an injury to his or her rights

precedent   A point of law that has been established and confirmed in a previous case, and which has bearing on the matter in hand

preponderance of the evidence   The greater weight of the evidence required in a civil (noncriminal) lawsuit to decide in favor of one side or the other; this preponderance is based on the more convincing evidence and its probable truth or accuracy, and not on the amount of evidence

pro bono   Legal work undertaken for no fee

probable cause   A reasonable belief that a person has committed a crime

spectral evidence   A form of evidence, accepted in court during the Salem Witch Trials, that was based upon dreams and visions

subornation   The act of inducing a person to commit perjury

Bibliography

Baden, Michael, and Judith Adler Hennessee. *Unnatural Death*. London: Sphere, 1991.

Baden, Michael, and Marion Roach, *Dead Reckoning: The New Science of Catching Killers*. New York: Simon & Schuster, 2001.

Bailey, F. Lee, and Harvey Aronson. *The Defense Never Rests*. New York: Stein & Day, 1971.

Baker, Liva. *Miranda: Crime, Law and Politics*. New York, Atheneum, 1983.

Blecker R. "A Verdict by Their Peers," *The Nation*. (October 3, 1987): 334ff.

Blaustein, Albert P, and Robert L. Zangrando. *Civil Rights and the American Negro*. New York: Trident, 1968.

Cagin, Seth, and Philip Dray. *We Are Not Afraid*. New York: Nation Books, 2006.

Cohn, Alfred, and Joe Chisholm. *Take the Witness*. New York: Frederick Stokes, 1934.

Cohn, Marjorie, and David Dow. *Cameras in the Courtroom*. Lanham, Md.: Rowman & Littlefield, 2002.

Evans, Colin. *Blood on the Table: The Greatest Cases of New York City's Office of the Chief Medical Examiner*. New York: Berkley, 2008.

Fletcher, George P. *A Crime of Self-Defense*. New York: Free Press, 1988.

Gaute, J. H. H., and Robin Odell. *Murder "Whatdunit."* London: Harrap, 1982.

Gaute, J. H. H., and Robin Odell. *The New Murderers' Who's Who*. New York: Dorset Press, 1979.

Gosch, Martin A., and Richard Hammer. *The Last Testament of Lucky Luciano*. Boston: Little, Brown, 1974.

Graham, Fred P. *The Self-Inflicted Wound*. New York, Macmillan Co., 1970

Grisham, John. *The Innocent Man*. New York: Doubleday, 2006.

Heimer, Mel. *The Cannibal*. New York: Windsor Pub., 1971.

Helpern, Milton, and Bernard Knight. *Autopsy*. London: Harrap, 1979.

Holmes, Paul. *The Sheppard Murder Case*. New York: McKay, 1961.

Houts, Marshall. *Where Death Delights*. New York: Coward-McCann, 1967.

Huie, William Bradford. *Three Lives for Mississippi*. Jackson, Miss.: University Press of Mississippi, 2000.

Jenkins, John A. *Ladies' Man: The Life and Trials of Marvin Mitchelson*. New York: St. Martin's Press, 1992.

Kilgallen, Dorothy. *Murder One*. New York: Random House, 1967.

Kornbluth, Jesse. "The Struggle Continues," *New York Times Magazine* (July 23, 1989): 16ff.

Knappman, Edward W., ed. *Great American Trials.* Detroit: Visible Ink, 1994.

Knappman, Edward W., ed. *Great World Trials.* Detroit: Visible Ink, 1997.

Kuntzler, William M. *The Minister and the Choir Singer.* New York: Morrow, 1964.

Lane, Brian. *Encyclopedia of Forensic Science.* London: Headline, 1992.

Lesly, Mark, and Charles Shuttleworth. *Subway Gunman.* Latham, N.Y.: British American Pub., 1988.

Lewis, Anthony. *Gideon's Trumpet.* New York: Random House, 1964

Lustgarten, Edgar. *Verdict in Dispute.* London: Wingate, 1949.

Marten, Manuel Edward. *The Doctor Looks at Murder.* Garden City, N.Y.: Doubleday, 1937.

Mauet, Thomas A. *Trials: Strategy, Skills, & New Powers of Persuasion.* Frederick, Md.: Aspen Publishers, 2009.

Neal, Bill. *Sex, Murder, and the Unwritten Law.* Lubbock, Tex.: Texas Tech University Press, 2009.

Noguchi, Thomas T., and Joseph DiMona. *Coroner.* Boston: G.K. Hall, 1984.

Noguchi, Thomas T., and Joseph DiMona. *Coroner at Large.* New York: Pocket Books, 1986.

Odell, Robin. *Science Against Crime.* London: Marshall Cavendish, 1982.

Peterson, Virgil W. *The Mob: 200 Years of Organized Crime in New York.* Ottawa, Ill.: Green Hill, 1983.

Pollack, Jack Harrison. *Dr Sam—An American Tragedy.* Chicago: Regnery, 1972.

Read, D. Shane. *Winning at Trial.* Denver: National Institute for Trial Advocacy, 2007.

Reuben, William A. *The Mark Fein Case.* New York: Dial Press, 1967.

Reynolds, Quentin. *Courtroom.* New York: Farrar, Strauss & Cudahy, 1940.

Saferstein, Richard. *Criminalistics: An Introduction to Forensic Science.* Upper Saddle River, N.J.: Prentice Hall, 1998.

Samaha, Joel. *Criminal Law.* Florence, Ky.: Wadsworth Publishing, 2007.

Scalia, Antonin, and Bryan A. Garner. *Making Your Case: The Art of Persuading Judges.* Eagan, Minn.: Thomson West, 2008.

Skene, William. "The Long Road Back," *National Review* (October 18, 1985): 28-35.

Spence, Gerry. *The Smoking Gun: Day by Day through a Shocking Murder Trial.* New York: Pocket Books, 2004.

Spence, Gerry. *Win Your Case.* New York: St. Martin's Griffin, 2006.

St. Johns, Adela Rogers. *Final Verdict.* New York: Doubleday, 1962.

Starkey, Marion L. *The Devil in Massachusetts.* Garden City, N.Y.: Doubleday, 1949.

Symons, Julian. *A Reasonable Doubt.* London: Cresset Press, 1960.

Thorwald, Jürgen. *The Century of the Detective.* New York: Harcourt, Brace & World, 1965.

Train, Arthur. *True Stories of Crime from the District Attorney's Office.* New York: Scribner's, 1908.

Trope, Mike. *Once upon a Time in Los Angeles: The Trials of Earl Rogers*. Spokane, Wash.: Clark Co., 2002.

Upham, Charles W. *Salem Witchcraft*. Williamstown, Mass. Corner House, 1971.

Villaseñor, Victor. *Jury: The* People vs. Juan Corona. Boston: Little, Brown, 1977.

Wecht, Cyril, Mark Curriden, and Benjamin Wecht. *Cause of Death*. New York: Dutton, 1993.

Wellman, Francis. *The Art of Cross Examination*. New York: Touchstone, 1997.

Wilson, Colin, and Patricia Pitman. *The Encyclopedia of Murder*. New York: Putnam's, 1962.

Wilson, Colin, and Donald Seaman. *The Encyclopedia of Modern Murder*. New York: Putnam's, 1983.

Further Resources

Books

Friedman, Lawrence M. *A History of American Law.* New York: Touchstone, 2005.

Langbein, John H., Renee Lettow Lerner, and Bruce P. Smith. *History of the Common Law.* New York: Wolters Kluwer Law & Business, 2009.

Mayo, Mike. *American Murder: Criminals, Crimes and the Media.* Detroit: Visible Ink, 2008.

Paternoster, Raymond, Robert Brame, and Sarah Bacon. *The Death Penalty: America's Experiences with Capital Punishment.* New York: Oxford University Press USA, 2007.

Paton, John and Angus Hall, eds., *Crimes and Punishment: A Pictorial Encylopedia of Aberrant Behavior.* Vols. 1–20. London: Phoebus Pub., 1974.

Schwartz, Bernard. *History of the Law in America.* New York: Heritage, 1974.

Web Sites

Gill, Kathy. "The Grand Jury in the United States," About.com.
URL: http://uspolitics.about.com/od/usgovernment/a/grand_jury.htm.
Accessed October 21, 2009.

Linder, Douglas. Famous Trials/University of Missouri Kansas City School of Law.
URL: http://www.law.umkc.edu/faculty/projects/ftrials/ftrials.htm.
Accessed October 21, 2009.

Supreme Court of the United States. Available online.
URL: http://www.supremecourtus.gov/index.html.
Accessed October 21, 2009.

Court Cases

Coleman v. State, 237 Ga. 84; 226 S.E.2d 911 (1976).

Isaacs v. State, 259 Ga. 717; 386 S.E.2d 316 (1989).

Isaacs v. State, 386 S.E.2d 316, Ga. (1989).

People v. Fein, 18 N.Y.2d 162; 219 N.E.2d 274; 272 N.Y.S.2d 753; 1966

Index

About the Author

Colin Evans is the author of numerous articles and books that deal with the history and development of forensic science. He has written *Blood on the Table: The Greatest Cases of New York City's Office of the Chief Medical Examiner*, *The Casebook of Forensic Detection*, *Criminal Investigations: Crime Scene Investigation*, and *The Father of Forensics: The Groundbreaking Cases of Sir Bernard Spilsbury and the Beginnings of Modern CSI*, and others. He lives in the United Kingdom. To find out more, visit his Web site at http://www.colin-evansonline.com